EARLY CHILDHOOD EDUCATION $

Leslie R. Williams, Editor   **Millie Almy, Senior Advisor**

ADVISORY BOARD: Barbara T. Bowman, Harriet K. Cuffaro, Stephanie Feeney, Doris Pronin Fromberg, Celia Genishi, Stacie G. Goffin, Dominic F. Gullo, Alice Sterling Honig, Elizabeth Jones, Gwen Morgan, David Weikart

(Continued)

Embracing Identities in Early Childhood Education

DIVERSITY AND POSSIBILITIES

EDITED BY
Susan Grieshaber
Gaile S. Cannella

Teachers College, Columbia University
New York and London

Published by Teachers College Press, 1234 Amsterdam Avenue, New York, NY 10027

Copyright © 2001 by Teachers College, Columbia University

Library of Congress Cataloging-in-Publication Data

Embracing identities in early childhood education : diversity and possibilities / edited by Susan Grieshaber, Gaile S. Cannella.
     p. cm. — (Early childhood education series)
    Includes bibliographical references and index.
    ISBN 0-8077-4079-9 (cloth : alk. paper) — ISBN 0-8077-4078-0 (pbk. : alk. paper)
     1. Early childhood education—Social aspects. 2. Postmodernism and education.
  I. Grieshaber, Susan. II. Cannella, Gaile Sloan, 1951– III. Early childhood education series (Teachers College Press)

  LB1139.23 .E58 2001
  372.21—dc21   00-067672

ISBN 0-8077-4078-0 (paper)
ISBN 0-8077-4079-9 (cloth)

Printed on acid-free paper
Manufactured in the United States of America

08 07 06 05 04 03 02 01   8 7 6 5 4 3 2 1

Contents

PART IV: Challenging Colonized Identities

Embracing Identities in Early Childhood Education

PART I

Exploring Reconceptualization in Early Childhood Education

From Identity to Identities: Increasing Possibilities in Early Childhood Education

Susan Grieshaber & Gaile S. Cannella

EMERGING BOTH GLOBALLY and locally, recent challenges to ways of understanding and living in the world have included issues of difference, identity, culture, intellect, and economy, as well as the construction of new technologies and reconceptualizations of the workplace. Early childhood educators have responded in various ways to such diversity. Many continue to support the developmentalist notion of the universal child. Others value more formal didactic approaches to their work with young children and their families. Still others merge a variety of perspectives in efforts to meet the challenges of diversity in its various forms.

Along with critiques of philosophy (e.g., Heidegger, 1977; Nietzsche, 1967) and the philosophy of science (e.g., Kuhn, 1970) have come critiques of dominant constructions of childhood (James, Jenks, & Prout, 1998). Further, critiques of early childhood education have challenged regimes of truth (Foucault, 1977) that privilege some children and marginalize others (Kessler, 1991; Lubeck, 1994; Walkerdine, 1984) and that normalize rather than celebrate and encourage difference (New & Mallory, 1994; Silin, 1995). Educators and researchers have been asked to rethink relationships with those who are younger in ways that recognize agency, voice, and complex identities, as well as a continued struggle for social justice (Cannella, 1997; Leavitt, 1994). This critical disposition has led to examination and *recon-ceptualization* of accepted ways of thinking about early childhood and associated practices of education and care. Some taken-for-granted ways of interpreting and practicing education are therefore being challenged and questioned.

Increasingly, we find in all avenues of our work (with young children and their families, teachers, and those completing teacher education programs) that there are no recipes or formulas on which we can rely. We believe that the world presently can be characterized by complexity, uncertainty, and questions of culture, difference, ethnicity, class, privilege, and politics (to name just a few). Young children, their families, and all of us are tied to these issues and others that are embedded within historical, social, and political circumstance.

The purpose of this book is to acknowledge our role as educators in the recognition of these human issues and the complex, dynamic identities emerging from them. One way in which we who work with young children can give voice to the complexity that constructs the human condition is to expand the range of perspectives possible for early childhood education. This expansion must go beyond dichotomous, truth-oriented thought to take on new and complex issues, to widen the arena of discourse(s) and action(s) available to early childhood educators. Although there are many understandings of the word *discourse*, we use it here in the same way that Best and Kellner (1991) describe discourse theory. That is, we are concerned with opening ways to

> analyze the institutional bases of discourse, the viewpoints and positions from which people speak, and the power relations these allow and presuppose. Discourse theory also interprets discourse as a site and object of struggle where different groups strive for hegemony [dominance] and the production of meaning and ideology. (p. 26)

As part of learning to live with complexity, uncertainty, and ambiguity, the authors in this book invite readers to explore the diversity in thought and practice that is occurring in the field, the reconceptualization of ways of knowing, listening to, being with, and educating young children. Part of what is shared in this book incorporates the exploration of institutional discourses such as the academy and the school, the positions from which people speak, and the power relations in which they are enmeshed.

Inspired by the work of those in philosophy, curriculum theory, women's studies, cultural studies, and postcolonial studies, the chapters in this volume focus on the shifting identities that characterize different ways of thinking about early childhood education in a *multicultural, changing, postmodern world*. The identities of children, families, teachers, researchers, and even early childhood education as a field are investigated from perspectives that generate possibilities for new and unthought-of ways of seeing, doing, and being in the world. This collection incorporates cutting-edge work that is being undertaken within the field, work that demonstrates how and why some are rejecting the dualistic thinking of oppositional concepts like appropriate/inappropriate, adult/child, work/play, or theory/practice. Further, this scholarship reveals that the field can respond/is responding to issues of difference, identity, social change, and politics.

Another way to address culture, privilege, politics, and changing conditions in the lives of young children and their families is to "question injustice and domination" (Popkewitz & Brennan, 1998, p. 29) and to illustrate how relying on one dominant way of thinking and understanding restricts possibilities and leads to greater oppression of children. The identity of the field of early childhood education at the present time is hierarchically tied to developmental psychology and its accompanying constructions of children and early education. More specifically, the dualistic understanding of developmentally appropriate and inappropriate practice dominates the field (and is even tied to government funding in some cases). The authors in this book present a range of identities that go beyond dualisms. They show that there is room in the field for more than the understandings of developmental psychology alone; this does not necessarily mean rejecting developmental psychology. Cases are made for understanding the field from a range of perspectives that encompass the significance of the local as well as the global; of culture, ethnicity, gender, and sexuality; of the historical and the political; and even of dominant scientific discourses. In other words, we are attempting to show that there are many identities that do/should constitute the field of early childhood education. To enable them to do this effectively, the authors have drawn on theoretical perspectives outside of developmental psychology and even outside of education. Their work is an acknowledgment that we need to incorporate a range of ways of theorizing and practicing to both celebrate and encourage diversity, as well as meet the challenges of changing times.

This first chapter begins with a brief overview of the *modernist* perspectives that have dominated the field of early childhood education. We then move to a description of *postmodern theories* or concepts that are either assumed or supported by many of the authors.

Modern and postmodern perspectives are discussed and related to the construction and perpetuation of identities in early childhood education.

Finally, the *reconceptualist* work of the authors found in this book is described. While acknowledging that some of the terms used here may be removed from the language of early childhood educators, we believe that the concepts discussed are part of the daily lives of most people. Ambiguity, uncertainty, and challenges to rationality (often referred to as conditions of postmodernity) are part of everyday experiences for all of us. Additionally, concepts associated with the postmodern are prevalent in the media, technology, and everyday conversations. Notably absent, however, is the language to accompany many of these everyday experiences, the lived complex identities that are part of all of our lives. In this book, the authors attempt to demonstrate the ways that reconceptualist, postmodernist perspectives can influence what we think and do in early childhood education, how opportunities and possibilities for young children can be achieved. While we are very aware of the difficulties of presenting theoretical concepts in ways that do not reduce complex ideas to simplistic notions, we have tried to resist the modernist temptation of generalizing. For this reason, we and the other authors in the book have tried to use examples to illustrate points.

MODERNIST THOUGHT: KNOWLEDGE, TRUTH, AND EDUCATION

Grounded in the Enlightenment search for universal human truths, the nineteenth and twentieth centuries have been labeled the period of modernization. The period is seen as such because of the contrast with the Middle Ages and feudalism. There were significant changes in society and culture, changes that included the development of science as truth, the belief in rational thought, and the separation of the mental from the physical.

Modernist knowledge is viewed as universal, predetermined, and to be discovered through empirically based science and technology. Associated with industrialization, secularism, and individualism, modernism perpetuates the belief in the truth of progress espoused by rationalist philosophers and applied to individuals, to civilizations, and to the discovery of knowledge. Reason (rationalism) is considered the avenue for discovering ways in which societies can achieve the goal of progress in all domains. Harvey (1989) noted that there are many debates about the meaning of the terms *modernism* and *moder-*

nity, but that the period is most often associated with "the belief in linear progress, absolute truths, the rational planning of ideal social orders, and the standardization of knowledge and production" (p. 9). According to Toulmin (1990), the Enlightenment project (modernism) was aimed at replacing the feudal system with a just and egalitarian society that valued reason and social progress.

Modernist thought fosters the belief in predetermined "truths" that exist in nature, prior to and independent of human beings, and that these truths can be discovered and understood through science. These "grand narratives" (Lyotard, 1984) are believed to reveal and explain the universal realities of life. Examples of modernist universal truths or grand narratives include notions of progress, individualism, rationality, the concrete/abstract learning dialectic, the elimination of poverty through technoindustrial development, and the Christian discourse of salvation. Developmental or child psychology has established itself as the grand narrative (also referred to as dominant discourse/universal truth) regarding those who are younger. This discourse, or universal way of thinking about children and education, has influenced child-rearing practices and pedagogy as well as exerted a powerful influence in the institutional field of early childhood education. Developmental psychology and the universal truth statements that it makes have not been questioned until recently. Early childhood scholars and even some developmental psychologists have used the work of Foucault to challenge universal perspectives, for example, the pre-existence of developmental structures (see, for example, Bloch, 1991; Burman, 1994).

Structuralism

Developmental psychology is a modern grand narrative that has a tendency to explain aspects of childhood through systems of meaning or structures that are pre-existing. This modern belief in prior structures (Hawkes, 1977), or systems of meaning, is termed *structuralism* and has been applied to elements that range from poems and novels to cognitive constructs like equilibration (Tobin, 1995). Freudian psychoanalysis, Sausserian linguistics, and Piagetian psychology all are structuralist theories.

The Piagetian (1964, 1968) perspective on learning as cognitive disequilibrium, concrete exploration, and concept construction is an example of a structural approach to human beings that is very influential in early childhood education. The structural system is believed to pre-exist for all people and to be universally applicable to intellect.

In relation to education, structuralism "promises accountability, efficiency, and control, as well as order, organization and certainty" (Cherryholmes, 1988, p. 30). Silin (1995) has drawn links between the dominance of Piaget's work in early childhood education and the particular type of culture in which we live. He says, "It is not surprising that Piaget's work, with its attention to rational modes of thought, has achieved wide popularity in a culture obsessed with technological accomplishments and scientific approaches to the management of human problems" (p. 90). This same notion of human structures has been/is responsible for the construction of human "identity" as a concept, as well as for the creation of individualistic and static interpretations of identity.

Individual Identities

Modernist theories position the individual or subject as "an unchanging human essence that preceded all social operations" (Best & Kellner, 1991, p. 51). This belief is consistent with modernist orientations toward universal truth—truth about individuals and even the knowledge, values, and attitudes that would constitute individuals. As the field of psychology emerged from Enlightenment/modernist beliefs about science and rational thought, a view of human beings as rational, unified, objective individuals developed. This true individual identity is considered able to transcend time and place and able to access what is considered by modernist theorists to be the real, true knowledge.

Adam, Henriques, Rose, Salfield, Venn, and Walkerdine (1977) identify two fundamental epistemological principles of the discipline of psychology. On the one hand, psychology claims to provide a general theory of human behavior. On the other, it claims to be a science of the individual. For psychology, then, to speak of the individual, is to speak of "man" in general—the social becomes a conglomeration of individuals and is explainable in terms of those individuals. The effect of this perspective is that the pre-given, unitary entity on which psychology is based makes the discipline itself both constitutive and productive. That is, a pre-existing truth about human beings is assumed by psychology, and therefore individuals are constructed and governed by that truth. As examples, a rational subject is presupposed, resulting in an identity that is based on the individual's "fit" with "rational" behavior. Progressive human development is accepted as truth, so those who are younger are constituted as immature, needing discipline, naive, and incompetent, as identities at the lower levels of a continuum created by the "truth" of progress. The practices and technologies that are centered on individualism actually construct and produce the individual itself and in the process inhibit alternative, counter-reproductive descriptions of identity and subjectivity (or ways of being).

However, counter identities do exist and have always existed. Contradictions to universal structures and truths emerge. This challenge was obvious in the late 1960s and 1970s when new political and intellectual movements, as well as cultural revolts, occurred "against a rigid and oppressive modern society" (Best & Kellner, 1991, p. ix). These revolts, combined with new technologies, media, computers, and changes in capitalism, paved the way for unthought-of ideas and ways of being, that is, for postmodernism.

POSTMODERNIST POSSIBILITIES

Although tied academically to various events over the past century and to shifts in thinking in a variety of fields, the term *postmodern* became prominent only in the 1980s and 1990s. Concern about the modernist belief in universal truths (grand narratives) and the imposition of those truths on all humanity have been expressed only recently (Lyotard, 1984). Although postmodernist perspectives could expand our ways of understanding each other and appreciating our differences, postmodernism is also undefinable and multidirectional and presents challenges to universal truths. The complexity, ambiguity, and certainly the challenge to truth are disturbing to many. We can describe postmodern positions as challenging ways of thinking that have dominated individual, group, and cultural beliefs about the world. In doing this, postmodern approaches use discourses that both accept and critique cultural practice. To consider the possibilities offered through philosophical perspectives that lean toward the postmodern, we must be willing to at least suspend our beliefs in universal truths. We must be able to view difference, complexity, and even confusion as part of everyday cultural and social life.

Challenges to Modernism

In contrasting modernism with postmodernism, Harvey (1989) stated that postmodernism "privileges heterogeneity and difference as liberative forces in the redefinition of cultural discourse. Fragmentation, indeterminacy, and intense distrust of all universal 'totalizing' discourses (to use the favored phrase) are the hallmark of postmodernist thought" (p. 9). Postmodern theory challenges the modernist belief that philosophical truths are the foundation for all knowledge and that these truths can be determined through approaches such as empiricism and rationalism. Postmodern thinking refutes modernist (positivist) claims that empirical observations can be used as proof for the truth of science. Further, postmodern thinking rejects rationalist premises that reason is the primary method of knowledge acquisition and that social and moral progress occurs through the rational application of social and scientific theories. In postmodern thinking, then, theories are viewed at best as providing "partial perspectives on their objects, and that all cognitive representations of the world are historically and linguistically mediated" (Best & Kellner, 1991, p. 4). Knowledge does not transcend perspective; rather, there are interpretations of interpretations.

Postmodernism is not a progressive next step beyond modernity, or a reaction to modernism. Postmodernism does, however, reject universalizing, truth-oriented perspectives that have privileged particular knowledge and groups of people. Postmodernism is boundless, messy, and ambiguous—as a view of the world, it opens doors to multiple new possibilities (Lather, 1991). Cannella and Bailey (1999) have provided an extensive discussion of postmodern work in the field of early childhood education that includes challenges to the child development and instructional knowledge bases that dominate the field, a critique of the construction of institutionalized power by professional organizations such as the National Association for the Education of Young Children, and an analysis of power positions for adults that emerge from the construction of "child" as the Other. Although modernist critiques have denounced postmodernism as providing only negative perspectives without actions that would change the field, we believe that a disposition that includes deconstruction, genealogical critique, and the recognition of social and political context is necessary in a field before reconceptualization and new possibilities can both emerge and gain support.

Deconstruction and Genealogical Critique

Two broad-based, historical research methods often used by postmodern scholars are deconstruction and genealogy. Deconstruction questions the assumption that modern science and philosophy can provide foundations for all knowledge (Derrida, 1976) or truth(s) that can be found to correctly explain philosophical systems (Best & Kellner, 1991). In her deconstruction of developmental psychology, Burman

(1994) described deconstruction as "laying bare, or bringing under scrutiny, the coherent moral-political themes that developmental psychology elaborates" (p. 1). Deconstruction reveals underlying values, biases, and beliefs that have generated particular views.

Genealogies, or genealogical critiques, are "historical analyses about how particular forms of reasoning and 'telling the truth' of the present involved shifts in the power relations and kinds of knowledge central to establishing a particular discourse" (Popkewitz & Brennan, 1998, p. 15). As part of her deconstruction of the discourse of early childhood education, Cannella (1997) undertook a genealogy of childhood in which she questioned the commonsense assumption that childhood is separate and quite different from adulthood. She concluded that childhood

> can be interpreted as a positivist construction that has dis-empowered younger human beings by creating them as incompetent and dependent on adults for care, knowledge and even bodily control. The discourses of childhood have fostered regulation of a particular group of human beings by another group (described as adults) and generated multiple sites of power for those adults. (p. 44)

Both deconstruction and genealogical critique involve an understanding of the interrelatedness of time, history, politics, context, social values, and human interpretations. These techniques and a variety of other methods and philosophical perspectives that challenge truth orientations (and would reveal marginalized knowledge) have been taken up by early childhood educators in their search for increased possibilities for young children, that is, in their reconceptualist endeavors.

Contemporary Reconceptualist Scholarship

Postmodern perspectives and other philosophical orientations that would challenge the existence and human application of universal truth (e.g., poststructuralism, feminism, queer theory, post- or neocolonialism) have led to reconceptualizations of the purposes for education and care, as well as the re-examination of research and practice. As examples, Robin Leavitt (1994) examined the ways in which infants and toddlers are physically and emotionally regulated through the policies and practices in child-care settings. In her study of power and resistance, she offered counter examples in which young children have more control over the choices that affect their bodies, minds, and lives. Joe Tobin (1997b) described work with student teachers in which they examined the fear of sexuality in preschool settings, revealing cultural differences in teacher expectations for normality, freedom of activity, and appropriate behavior for young children.

Other contemporary work related to early childhood education includes the work of *poststructuralists* who have critiqued structuralist beliefs in pre-existing systems of meaning. An illustration is the poststructuralist work that challenges child development and other scientific claims to universal cognitive structures. Burman (1994) argues that the focus on the individual child as a unit of analysis in and of itself removes child development from any historical and social conditions. Thus the individual child, as the point of analysis for developmental psychology, is ahistorical, asocial, and apolitical. The normalized understandings that are an integral part of child development serve to mark any difference from the idealized norm as if it were a deficiency.

Concerned with the lives of women, *feminist* poststructuralists have called into question regimes of truth that dictate life roles and expectations and have critiqued the relationships among gender, power, and education. Bronwyn Davies's (1991) exploration of the gendered expectations of preschool children illustrates this perspective, as does her examination of how and why children become masculine and feminine (Davies, 1989). The latter provides a detailed account of the gendered world of children aged 4 and 5 and how their gendered identities are socially constructed as an integral part of their everyday lives.

Closely tied to feminism and poststructuralism, *queer theory* challenges both specific and generally accepted constructions of gender and identity. For example, Valerie Walkerdine (1990) examined the ways that female identities are constructed to accept masculine teaching beliefs. Tobin (1997a) described queer theory as "an emerging reworking of gay and lesbian theory and political action that integrates elements of poststructuralism, feminism, gender studies, and cultural studies" (p. 26). Tobin also argued for "queering up early childhood education" (p. 26). By this he means "not only paying attention to gay and lesbian perspectives in our research on young children but more generally calling into question 'the regime of the normal'" (p. 26).

Perhaps most recently, the voices of *postcolonial* or *neocolonial* scholars are emerging related to and from early childhood education. Although physical appropriation of land and lives is now less common, intellectual and economic colonization is increasing (Viruru & Cannella, 1999). Further, over 80% of the globe experienced the effects of modern European colonialism (Fieldhouse, 1989) during the nine-teenth century, resulting in a massive number of people of all ages who in some form or another have experienced (and currently live with the effects of) colonization. Postcolonial research explores the lives, work, and perspectives of colonized and diasporic peoples. An example of this scholarship is the work of Radhika Viruru (in press), who explores early childhood education in India, including the more indigenous curriculum and views of being with children as well as the effects of the "empire."

These postmodern perspectives have begun to reveal the diversity in thinking and action that previously have been marginalized in childhood education—voices of those who do not fit psychological constructions of development and reason, voices of those whose cul-tural strengths have been labeled as underdeveloped and savage, voices of those who have been stigmatized as illegitimate, as not nor-mal. As these voices are heard, they provide challenges to the identi-ties that we have held sacred, the predetermined, truth-oriented identi-ties that we have cherished for ourselves as teachers and human beings, the identities that we as adults have constructed for children, and even the identity of the field of early childhood education.

POSTMODERN SHIFTING IDENTITIES

The notion of identity associated with modernist understandings of the world is singular and unitary. A postmodern understanding of identities is that they are multiple and complex, and even changing (and that even the concept of identity is, most likely, a cultural, sci-entifically oriented construction that probably would not exist in all cultures and times). Although there are a variety of theoretical per-spectives from which to draw understandings, a postmodern under-standing of identities moves beyond dualisms like good/bad, male/female, masculine/feminine, mature/immature, or even appropriate/inappropriate. Through the historical critique of psychology and other institutionalized societal discourses, postmodern theories offer an un-derstanding of the subject as "socially and linguistically decentered and fragmented" (Best & Kellner, 1991, p. 5). In this understanding, subjects (people) or subjectivities are seen to be dynamic and multiple, and always positioned in relation to particular discourses and the practices produced by the discourses.

Postmodern perspectives argue for the acceptance of multiple and contradictory identities. For example, in a feminist poststructuralist understanding there can be no ultimate fixing of femininity or masculinity. Identities "are always historically produced through a range of discursive practices" (Weedon, 1997, p. 146), with change over time and in different situations. This means that there are no essential feminine or masculine attributes that are consistent across all histories and contexts. Likewise, there are no pre-existing child or adult characteristics that represent truth regardless of circumstance. Hatch (1995) explains:

> There is no permanent and essential nature of childhood. The idea of childhood is defined differently in every culture, in every time period, in every political climate, in every economic era, in every social context. Our everyday assumption that the childhood we "know" is and always has been *the* definition of childhood turns out to be false. (p. 118)

Postmodern perspectives challenge the existence of essentialized individual or educational identities, whether for those who are young, for parents and teachers, or for the values, knowledges, and methods of the field of early childhood education.

Psychology and developmental psychology are historically embedded in an initial concern with control and surveillance of the general population (Walkerdine, 1984), the production and control of particular identities. As a field, and fostered by patriarchal and power-oriented perspectives in society, psychology has constructed discourses that make possible techniques of discipline and regulation of human beings. These disciplinary powers (Foucault, 1978) create standards through which identities are constructed, and judgment and categorization by society are legitimized. We have already referred to discourses of rational and progressive identities. Another example includes the discourse of woman as mother, where all those identified as "woman" (another disciplinary identity) are assumed to naturally want to have and nurture children. Marshall (1991) discusses the social construction of motherhood through an analysis of parenting manuals, showing that motherhood is constructed as "ultimate fulfillment" (p. 68) and that mother love is understood as natural. Further, Marshall argues that the manuals place responsibility on mothers for the

> "normal development" of a well-adjusted individual. To mother adequately a woman needs to be present with her child 24 hours each day and to be continually and actively engaged, providing stimulating and attentive company. If her child's development is not normal, the blame falls on the mother. . . . Another implicit consequence is to level the responsibility for the next generation's moral welfare on individual women's shoulders and

to locate any social problems in faulty mothering. Again, society and structural influences are omitted from the equation. (p. 83)

This is an example of how a disciplinary power is concealed in the language of "natural and good mothering," creating a disciplinary identity for all mothers. It follows that those who do not yield to the dominant discourse can be labeled as semi-woman and pervert, thus legitimating the dominant discourse (Cherniavsky, 1995; Eyer, 1992; Welter, 1979).

Specifically related to early childhood education, the dominant discourse of developmentally appropriate practice (DAP) (Bredekamp, 1987; Bredekamp & Copple, 1997) constructs the identity of the good early childhood practitioner. The discourse creates both the desire to be the good teacher and a definition of the good teacher in DAP terms. Good practitioners are constituted and regulated within the claims of developmentally appropriate practice and learn to judge themselves as "good" or "bad" teachers according to that discourse. This facet of developmental psychology is discussed in Chapter 2 of this volume, "Personal Stories," where a number of perspectives are provided from people who have questioned this dominant discourse in early childhood education. These personal stories explain reasons for challenging developmentally appropriate practice and outline paths taken in quests for other ways of understanding children, childhood, and early childhood curriculum and practice.

The authors whose work is presented in Parts II–IV of this volume have accepted the challenge to move beyond pre-existing, truth-oriented identities. Their work acknowledges the ways in which modernist discourses have constituted, regulated, and limited identity, even as they explore ways of reconstituting identities, of creating shifts in perspective that increase acceptance and life possibilities for all those involved in our educational endeavors. The chapters are categorized under three broad constructions: (1) the ways that education has limited teaching identities and the conceptualization of avenues for the creation of counter identities, (2) the reconceptualization of multiple and new identities (for individuals and even concepts within the field) through diverse cultural representations, and (3) challenges to the colonized identities that dominate educational practice.

Counter Identities: Constructions That Limit Education

In Part II of the book, the authors reveal the narrow and simplistic identities that have been constructed for the teacher in early childhood

education, through developmental, "good" teacher, and even recon-
structionist discourses. This work demonstrates the complexity of
teacher identities, the global and local contexts in which teacher identities are constructed, and the ways in which counter and multidirectional perspectives can generate new possibilities for practice.

In Chapter 3, Sharon Ryan, Mindy Ochsner, and Celia Genishi explore the loss to children and the field when teachers and instructional
methodologies are constructed as either developmentally appropriate
or inappropriate. The authors probe research on teaching, a major vehicle for the production of teacher images. Representations of teaching
and early childhood teachers produced within historically dominant
forms of research are juxtaposed with images created by poststructuralist studies of early childhood education. By exploring research on
teaching at both the center and the poststructuralist margins, the authors demonstrate the limitations of dominant approaches to early
childhood research and the possibilities constructed through research
agendas that are more critically focused. Poststructuralism is viewed
as offering more complex interpretations (or readings) of what it means
to be an early childhood teacher and greater possibilities for the prob-
lematization (within political, historical, and dominated contexts) of
everyday conceptions of teacher identities and practices.

Another way in which teacher identities can be understood as
more complex than the dualism generated through developmentally
appropriate versus inappropriate discourse is by examining the literature on advocacy in early childhood education. For some time, early
childhood literature has supported the idea that educators should be
activists for young children, their families, and the profession. In
Chapter 4, Susan Grieshaber uses a feminist poststructuralist position
to explore the ways in which early childhood educators are positioned
through advocacy literature and through the dominant discourse of
early childhood education that is developmentally appropriate practice. The advocacy literature constructs educators as confrontational,
demanding, willing to engage in conflict, and open to both critique
and negotiation. However, developmentally appropriate practice positions teachers as those who quietly respond as caring, nurturing, and
facilitative of children's development. Connections between these two
bodies of literature are examined to reveal human ambiguity and multiple identities, the complexity that is integral to all early childhood
educators.

Janice Kroeger has called into question the regime of the normal
in Chapter 5. In her autobiographical, multinarrative text of a bisexual
teacher, Kroeger describes how she attempts to include a lesbian fam-

ily into a rural early childhood program. The tale is a collaboratively driven narrative that exposes dilemmas in teaching, and challenges assumptions concerning teacher determination of family and child needs. Further, the tale reveals the complexity and social embeddedness of identity and educational practices. Although identified as a transformational teacher, upon observing the family/community experience, Kroeger questions her own identity as an activist for "others." The chapter is in fellowship with a growing body of work that addresses the concerns of gay/lesbian/bisexual and transgendered (GLBT) teachers, students, and families.

RECONCEPTUALIZED IDENTITIES: EXPANDING CULTURAL REPRESENTATIONS

In Part III the authors explore possibilities for reinventing and expanding the various identities that characterize individuals and the field of early childhood education. The multiple identities include reconceptualization of what is meant by (1) observation, (2) the biases within gendered language that assumes heterosexuality as the norm in the early childhood classroom, and (3) possibilities for using the complexities of corporate marketing and popular culture to develop critical dispositions with young children. Each of these reconceptualizations results in the generation of new identities for educational/care content and practice.

Writing from a feminist poststructuralist position, Sheralyn Campbell and Kylie Smith provide two interpretations (or readings) of child observation in an early childhood setting (Chapter 6). An extended interaction among three children (two girls and one boy) in a construction-site play area is interpreted using both developmental and feminist poststructuralist discourses. Developmental readings of the situation reveal normalized children who are placed in particular positions regarding social, language, and cognitive skills, interpreted as varying in social negotiation abilities and labeled as imitating the behavior of others. A feminist poststructuralist reading reveals human beings who are gendered in behavior and in attempts to exercise or maintain power. One child even functions as the silent "other" to avoid exclusion and to support the teacher's developmental discourse (a position that denies a political, contextual link between gendered discourses and individuals). The authors demonstrate that all our observations are grounded within particular views of the world that limit what is "seen" and must be examined for what is ignored.

In Chapter 7, Rachel Theilheimer and Betsy Cahill address the notion of sexuality. The authors construct a metaphorical closet within early childhood education that houses beliefs about sexuality. These beliefs include the construction of children as asexual, innocent beings within educational practices that produce heteronormativity, the assumption that the "normal" state of being human is heterosexual. The authors illustrate the ways in which educators and parents underestimate what children know and understand, and how children accept and appreciate what adults try to avoid. Heteronormative presentations and dialogue in early childhood classrooms (e.g., romantic pairing of little girls and boys, statements such as "children don't become gay or lesbian by playing dress-up") are examined as establishing an atmosphere in which homophobia and heterosexist behavior dominate.

In Chapter 8, Patrick Hughes and Glenda Mac Naughton use the considerable international debate over the influence of *Barbie* play on the sense of self and gendering identities of young children to propose a poststructuralist understanding of identity formation. In this understanding, individuals assemble their own discursive repertoires by adopting one or more discourses circulating within the social arena. The poststructuralist model proposes that some discourses have been institutionalized within the cultural product and communication industries. Barbie is discussed as a cultural product whose influence is grounded in the domination and power produced by these discourses. Teachers are advised to establish an environment of critique with children in which the products of corporations and popular culture are examined.

Challenging Colonized Identities

The authors in Part IV object to the imposition of colonization and colonizing constructs (i.e., individualism, minority, research) and to the constituting of identities through these constructs in education. They listen to Māori, Japanese American, Indian, and other oppressed and colonized voices that would question Enlightenment, dualistic identities.

In Chapter 9 Jenny Ritchie proposes that a counter-pervasiveness of collectivity, illustrated in the Māori focus on extended family, be adopted by early childhood educators. In New Zealand, educators are facing an extremist ideology in the form of New Right individualism that seeks to remove government from sharing responsibility for nurturing young children and families. The focus on collectivity is found within the context of the early childhood curriculum designed for New Zealand, *Te Whāriki*. The philosophy is explained by focusing on the Māori extended family (*whānau*), the work of feminists such as Nel Noddings, and the sociocultural perspectives emphasized by Vygotsky.

In Chapter 10, Susan Matoba Adler provides the self-reflection of a Japanese American scholar-educator attending an early childhood education reconceptualist conference in Honolulu. Adler examines how the process of interacting professionally and personally and the sharing of individual responses to significant events created a discourse for reconceptualizing her own teacher identities and voices. She describes how, as an individual, she came to the conference with perspectives on her own experiences and research, yet left with a rich understanding of how frames of reference may be interpreted differently by other scholars. Adler explains conference activities in which she, as a Japanese American, experienced the oppression of other ethnic groups as imposed by Japanese American dominance. She further describes how her own conceptions of Asian American oppression and visibility, within the sociopolitical context of White dominance and Black/White dichotomy, were challenged.

As the objects of research practices, children have been marginalized and disqualified from having voices, as they rarely are consulted about their participation in research projects. In Chapter 11, Radhika Viruru and Gaile Cannella critique the notion of research from a neocolonial perspective (as they attempt to listen to the voices of adults and children in India). The authors explain a postcolonial understanding that acknowledges the continued effects of colonizing through discursive practices and philosophical domination. Within this perspective, the construct of the universal child is examined as unrestrictedly colonizing. Even qualitative ethnographic study with children is revealed as hierarchical, undemocratic, creating power for the researcher, and embedded within voyeuristic, truth-oriented assumptions. Viruru and Cannella ask, "What are the ways in which early childhood curriculum reflects imperialist assumptions about and misrepresentations of historically colonized peoples? (quoting Cannella & Bailey, 1999, p. 23)" and "How does one co-construct a new kind of research with children that reflects their perspectives?" Based on these questions, the authors present a number of reconceptualizations of researching with children.

The concluding chapter of the book draws together the major contributions of each chapter for theory and practice, highlights ongoing identity issues of concern for early childhood educators, and ties these issues to reconceptualizations of the field. We encourage the reader to explore ways of reconstituting identities, of creating shifts in perspective that increase acceptance and life possibilities for all those involved in our educational endeavors.

REFERENCES

Adam, D., Henriques, J., Rose, N., Salfield, A., Venn, C., & Walkerdine, V. (1977). Psychology, ideology and the human subject. *Ideology and Consciousness, 1*, 5–56.

Best, S., & Kellner, D. (1991). *Postmodern theory: Critical interrogations.* London: Macmillan.

Bloch, M. N. (1991), Critical social science and the history of child development's influence on early education research. *Early Education and Development, 2*(2), 95–108.

Bredekamp, S. (1987). *Developmentally appropriate practice in early childhood programs serving children from birth through age 8.* Washington, DC: National Association for the Education of Young Children.

Bredekamp, S., & Copple, C. (1997). *Developmentally appropriate practice in early childhood programs serving children from birth through age 8* (rev. ed.). Washington, DC: National Association for the Education of Young Children.

Burman, E. (1994). *Deconstructing developmental psychology.* London: Routledge.

Cannella, G. S. (1997). *Deconstructing early childhood education: Social justice and revolution.* New York: Peter Lang.

Cannella, G. S., & Bailey, C. D. (1999). Postmodern research in early childhood education. In S. Reifel (Ed.), *Advances in early education and day care* (Vol. 10, pp. 3–39). Greenwich, CT: JAI Press.

Cherniavsky, E. (1995). *That pale mother rising: Sentimental discourses and the imitation of motherhood in nineteenth century America.* Bloomington: Indiana University Press.

Cherryholmes, C. (1988). *Power and criticism: Poststructural investigations in education.* New York: Teachers College Press.

Davies, B. (1989). *Frogs and snails and feminist tales: Preschool children and gender.* North Sydney, NSW: Allen & Unwin.

Davies, B. (1991). The accomplishment of genderedness in pre-school children. In L. Weis, P. G. Altbach, G. P. Kelly, & H. G. Petrie (Eds.), *Critical perspectives in early childhood education* (pp. 83–100). Albany: State University of New York Press.

Derrida, J. (1976). *Of grammatology.* Baltimore: Johns Hopkins University Press.

Eyer, D. E. (1992). *Mother–infant bonding: A scientific fiction.* New Haven: Yale University Press.

Fieldhouse, D. K. (1989). *The colonial empires*. London: Macmillan.

Foucault, M. (1977). *Discipline and punish: The birth of the prison* (A. Sheridan, Trans.). Harmondsworth, England: Penguin.

Foucault, M. (1978). *The history of sexuality* (Vols. I–III). New York: Pantheon.

Harvey, D. (1989). *The condition of postmodernity: An enquiry into the origins of cultural change*. Oxford: Basil Blackwell.

Hatch, J. A. (1995). Studying childhood as a cultural invention: A rationale and framework. In J. A. Hatch (Ed.), *Qualitative research in early childhood settings* (pp. 117–133). Westport, CT: Praeger.

Hawkes, T. (1977). *Structuralism and semiotics*. London: Methuen.

Heidegger, M. (1977). *The question concerning technology*. New York: Harper & Row.

James, A., Jenks, C., & Prout, A. (1998). *Theorizing childhood*. New York: Teachers College Press.

Kessler, S. (1991). Alternative perspectives in early childhood education. *Early Childhood Research Quarterly, 6*, 183–197.

Kuhn, T. S. (1970). *The structure of scientific revolutions* (2nd ed.). Chicago: University of Chicago Press.

Lather, P. (1991). *Getting smart: Feminist research and pedagogy with/in the postmodern*. New York: Routledge.

Leavitt, R. L. (1994). *Power and emotion in infant–toddler day care*. Albany: State University of New York Press.

Lubeck, S. (1994). The politics of developmentally appropriate practice. In B. L. Mallory & R. S. New (Eds.), *Diversity and developmentally appropriate practices: Challenges for early childhood education* (pp. 17–39). New York: Teachers College Press.

Lyotard, J. (1984). *The postmodern condition: A report on knowledge* (G. Bennington & B. Massumi, Trans.). Minneapolis: University of Minnesota Press.

Marshall, H. (1991). The social construction of motherhood: An analysis of childcare and parenting manuals. In A. Phoenix, A. Woollett, & E. Lloyd (Eds.), *Motherhood: Meanings, practices and ideologies* (pp. 66–85). London: Sage.

New, R. S., & Mallory, B. L. (1994). Introduction: The ethic of inclusion. In B. L. Mallory & R. S. New (Eds.), *Diversity and developmentally appropriate practices: Challenges for early childhood education* (pp. 1–13). New York: Teachers College Press.

Nietzsche, F. (1967). *The will to power*. New York: Random House.

Piaget, J. (1964). *The early growth of logic in the child*. New York: Harper.

Piaget, J. (1968). *The psychology of intelligence*. Totowa, NJ: Littlefield, Adams.

Popkewitz, T., & Brennan, M. (1998). Restructuring of social and political theory in education: Foucault and a social epistemology of school practices. In T. Popkewitz & M. Brennan (Eds.), *Foucault's challenge: Discourse, knowledge, and power in education* (pp. 3–35). New York: Teachers College Press.

Silin, J. G. (1995). *Sex, death, and the education of children: Our passion for ignorance in the age of AIDS*. New York: Teachers College Press.

Tobin, J. (1995). Post-structural research in early childhood education. In J. A. Hatch (Ed.), *Qualitative research in early childhood settings* (pp. 223–243). Westport, CT: Praeger.

Tobin, J. (1997a). The missing discourse of pleasure and desire. In J. Tobin (Ed.), *Making a place for pleasure in early childhood education* (pp. 1–38). New Haven, CT: Yale University Press.

Tobin, J. (1997b). Playing doctor in two cultures: The United States and Ireland. In J. Tobin (Ed.), *Making a place for pleasure in early childhood education* (pp. 119–158). New Haven: Yale University Press.

Toulmin, S. (1990). *Cosmopolis: The hidden agenda of modernity*. New York: Free Press.

Viruru, R. (in press). *Decolonizing early childhood education: An Indian perspective*. New Delhi: Sage.

Viruru, R., & Cannella, G. S. (1999, October). *A postcolonial scrutiny of early childhood education*. Presented at the meeting of the Journal of Curriculum Theorizing Conference, Dayton, OH.

Walkerdine, V. (1984). Developmental psychology and the child-centered pedagogy: The insertion of Piaget into early childhood education. In J. Henriques, W. Holloway, C. Urwin, C. Venn, & V. Walkerdine (Eds.), *Changing the subject: Psychology, social regulation and subjectivity* (pp. 153–202). London: Methuen.

Walkerdine, V. (1990). *Schoolgirl fictions*. London: Verso.

Weedon, C. (1997). *Feminist practice and poststructuralist theory* (2nd ed.). Oxford: Basil Blackwell.

Welter, B. (1979). The cult of true womanhood: 1820–1860. In L. Dinnerstein & K. Jackson (Eds.), *American vistas (1607–1877)* (pp. 176–198). New York: Oxford University Press.

CHAPTER 2

Personal Stories: Early Childhood Educators and Reconceptualized Identities

Gaile S. Cannella & Susan Grieshaber

MANY OF US who have chosen to work in early childhood, whatever our philosophical persuasion, have at least one characteristic in common. We are concerned about the lives, care, and education of those who are younger. Whether we cling to behavioral views of learning, believe in universal child development, or have found that we would challenge all theories about human beings in the name of diversity and equity, we want to serve other human beings.

In recent years (as the feud between behavioral and developmental perspectives has continued in classrooms), two groups of early childhood educational researchers have emerged. Generally opposing extreme behaviorism, one group is tied to developmental psychology and the belief that Piagetian perspectives create more humane, fair, and natural environments for all children. This group has become highly associated with the National Association for the Education of Young Children (in the United States) and its push for developmentally appropriate practice in early childhood classrooms. These developmental perspectives are being used for accreditation of programs and for construction of concepts of "good teaching," and are even tied to government funding in some cases. Although we would not assume to speak accurately for any entire group of people or individuals, our own experiences with child development lead us to believe that many of the educators who strongly believe in universal child development believe that understanding and using developmental perspectives in classrooms improves the lives and learning of young children; that some believe that parents can learn to understand their children better through child development; and that many believe that children are treated with more respect and given more freedom and opportunities through child development. Developmentalists genuinely want the best for all children.

The second group that has emerged are those who have grown concerned about diverse ways of living, learning, and being in the world. Generally experienced in developmental psychology, many in this group have come to believe that any "truth," whether behavioral, developmental, or other, that would be imposed on everyone is dangerous—is damaging to at least a few if not many. Those that challenge the truth(s) of child development, and even the creation of "children" as a separate group from "adults," sometimes have labeled themselves (and also may be labeled by others) as reconceptualists, postmodernists, feminist poststructuralists, and on and on. These philosophical characterizations have come from fields outside of early childhood education and developmental psychology, as these early childhood educators have struggled to learn about the lives and experiences of others. Many of them believe that younger human beings are not separate from the historical, political, and social context in which they live (or the issues of gender, race, socioeconomic level, or power that are part of time and context); they believe that younger human beings and their families (especially if they are not part of the dominant power elite) have not been listened to or even respected as having identities or voice; they believe that engaging in the human struggle to make unthought-of connections with each other may increase life possibilities for all of us. As more identified with this reconceptualist group in recent years, we know that we and our colleagues also are genuinely concerned for other human beings.

However, we identify somewhat different issues as most prominent in human life than do the developmentalists. We approach our work with those who are younger using different philosophical frameworks and beliefs about human beings. We do not propose that our perspectives are a "truth," or the "correct" way of viewing the world; in our work, we try to challenge that need for a truth. We do believe (as a shared value rather than a truth) that all perspectives must be heard, understood, and respected. However, we also believe that all views of the world must be historically examined and deconstructed. From within any set of beliefs, the questions must be asked: Who is helped? Who gains power? Whose knowledge is privileged? Who is hurt? Who is disqualified? Yet, we also hope to continually challenge the biases within the questions that we raise. This is also a genuine concern for diverse human beings, diverse voices, and the power that allows some to be heard and not others.

Unfortunately, using language to describe the two groups, developmentalists and reconceptualists, creates a dichotomy that may not really exist. The groups share similar backgrounds in education and classroom practices, many of the same cultural experiences, and, most important, genuine concern for other human beings. Additionally, we believe that as human beings who want to be open to diversity, we should respect diverse perspectives and forms of meaning making. For these reasons, we hope to expand our field by making connections with all who are part of it and with people who share the lives of children but who have not always been heard as part of a field like early childhood education. Further, we would challenge the boundaries of our own field, expanding the limits by listening to the daily life experiences and interpretations of others and listening to diverse understandings of being in the world that come from different cultures, races, gendered experiences, sexual orientations, and socioeconomic conditions.

One way to expand the field of possibilities and make connections with others is to begin by sharing our own personal stories, our stories of everyday life as people and as educators. These stories reveal how we connect our work with young children to theory, practice, and daily actions; to lived worlds of oppression and inequity; and to worlds of hope and possibility. The following are the personal/professional stories of five early childhood educators. Some feel comfortable labeling themselves as reconceptualists, feminists, or poststructuralists; others do not. Some stories are individual; others are grounded in years of collective professional activity. Each story provides a somewhat different path and focus on reconceptualization and postmodernism. We invite you to become personally involved with these stories, to examine your own personal/professional identities, and to generate new possibilities.

QUESTIONING ASSUMPTIONS

By J. Amos Hatch

I came to early childhood education late in my undergraduate experience. I was a rising senior in political science at the University of Utah, planning to do law school or go into the diplomatic corps, when I took an introduction to education course to fill hours during the summer. The instructor sent us to several education settings available that summer—remedial programs in public schools, the local Job Corps, and a Head Start center. I remember sitting in the back of the Head Start classroom when a tiny, African American girl with thick, long braids came over to me and lifted her arms in a gesture that said pick me up. I did, and that moment changed my life. I became a volunteer at the center, organized a volunteer program for other university students, and eventually changed my major. During the remainder of my time at the university, I spent more time at the Head Start center than on campus, and my career objective was to become a Head Start teacher.

My degree from Utah was in elementary education because I could complete it much sooner than if I had gone for a degree from the College of Home Economics. I moved to Kansas City, Missouri, after graduation and took a job as a second-grade teacher in a behavior analysis Follow-Through program in the inner city. So my (accelerated) teacher training was in a college of education that emphasized a humanistic approach, and my first job was in a school that required the strict implementation of a program based on behaviorist learning principles. I knew something of developmental psychology and the early childhood pedagogy of the day, but I was so into being with kids that I really never examined my own beliefs about learning, teaching, and development. After 2 years, I moved to Jacksonville, Florida, where once again I lived and worked in the inner city, this time teaching in a unique K–2 program for children who were struggling but did not qualify for special education. In Jacksonville, I started a master's program in elementary/early childhood education. I learned a lot about early childhood theory, foundations, and curriculum, but my primary aim was to do a better job as a practicing teacher.

Beginning a Ph.D. program at the University of Florida brought on another life-changing realization. Rodman Webb's social foundations class at UF slapped me in the face. I had never thought seriously about the idea that schools were institutions responsible for socializing the next generation. I had never contemplated the conflicting forces that seek to determine what schools ought to be like and who ought to be successful there. I had never considered the possibility that schools served the social, political, and economic ends of those in power. By now, I was a die-hard developmentalist in the Piagetian tradition, and I remember doing a book report on Richard de Lone's *Small Futures* (1979) that forced me to re-examine my assumptions about how children develop. I still have the paper that I turned in to Professor Webb.

I blew off de Lone's argument for a "situational theory of child development," including the idea that development was different for children of poverty than for more privileged children, referencing my knowledge of Piaget's universal stage theory. Webb did not blast my thinking; he just wrote in the margin next to my description of de Lone's situational thesis, "I think this is one of his best points! I don't think we pay enough attention to differences in social class." That sent me back to the book and forward to an exploration of other unexamined assumptions I was carrying around. I was hardly a critical theorist, but I did find lots of insight in the work of Bowles and Gintis and Henry Giroux that had me thinking more broadly about education and opportunity in our society.

I also became interested in qualitative research at Florida, and again Rodman Webb sparked my interest. I rejected positivist science, did a qualitative dissertation study in a kindergarten classroom, and set about building a career as an early childhood qualitative researcher. I became a foot soldier in the paradigm wars of the 1980s and 1990s. A big part of my conversion to qualitative research involved unpacking my own assumptions and challenging the taken-for-granted premises of traditional research in education. I also looked outside the developmental psychology canon for the substantive theory that would inform my research in early childhood settings, choosing instead to present my findings within frameworks from sociology and social psychology. So, my own intellectual journey through my doctoral program led me into a pattern of questioning assumptions, challenging what is taken for granted, and considering alternative ways of conceptualizing ideas. After graduation, I taught early childhood courses at Ohio State University's Marion campus for 3 years, then continued doing so at the University of Tennessee at Knoxville. For several years, my teaching looked pretty much like what I had experienced in my early childhood coursework, heavily emphasizing Piaget, developmental psychology, and the developmentally appropriate practices of the National Association for the Education of Young Children. After moving to Tennessee, I was invited to edit a special issue on early childhood research for *Qualitative Studies in Education*. As part of the project, I organized a conference that brought together many of the individuals who were doing qualitative work in early childhood. The meetings were a terrific experience, and folks left with the feeling that other opportunities should be created for individuals to get together who operate outside the mainstream of early childhood education. Some of those folks joined with others to start the early childhood reconceptualizing group that has met for the past several years.

My participation in the reconceptualizing group and my association with the innovative thinkers in the group have led me to continue
to question and look for alternatives to the taken-for-granted in our
field. I have not become a poststructuralist, a feminist, or a critical
theorist, but I admire much of the work done in these fields of inquiry.
I am intrigued with what early childhood educators can learn from
opening ourselves to these sometimes troubling perspectives. In much
of my professional work, I see myself as a kind of mediator between
the mainstream and my "radical" friends. In my teaching and scholarship, I try to introduce alternative thinking into the discourse that
dominates early childhood scholarship and practice, without damning
that discourse out of hand. I try to participate in reconceptualizing
activities in ways that remind my colleagues that unless what we do
serves to bring about positive changes for children, families, and teachers, we are only talking to ourselves.

Most early childhood educators come to the field because of feelings like those I experienced at the Salt Lake Head Start Center. Our
roots may be in different philosophical, theoretical, or political soil,
but we care deeply about kids and those responsible for their learning
and development. Disagreements are inevitable, but that's a good
thing, even in a profession that loves harmony. It's healthy for our
field to come at important issues from different perspectives as long
as we are doing everything possible, using every tool available, and
forming every alliance we can in a concerted effort to improve the life
chances for children.

ALL THE CHILDREN IN THE WORLD:
WHY I BECAME A RECONCEPTUALIST

By Janice A. Jipson

Officially, it all began in New Orleans in 1987. Shirley Kessler and I
were attending the American Educational Research Association (AERA)
conference and had slipped out of a session to commiserate with each
other about academic life. The conversation turned to "developmentally appropriate practice" and the seemingly universal acceptance by
the early childhood community of child development theory as the
basis for early childhood curriculum. Our discussion had begun much
earlier, however. As graduate students at the University of Wisconsin–
Madison, we often had shared our concerns about the increasing dominance of the child development perspective in our field and specu-
lated as to what an early childhood curriculum grounded in critical

theory might be. The Reconceptualizing Early Childhood Education movement of the 1990s had emerged out of these earlier conversations (Jipson & Johnson, 2000).

When Gaile Cannella invited me to write about why I had become involved in the reconceptualization of early childhood education, I first thought back to my graduate school days and my work in critical theory with Professor Michael Apple where I had first undertaken a formal critique of direct instruction. Psychologically framed models of early childhood had long been a concern of mine. Even as an undergraduate student in Harry Harlow's introductory psychology course, I found behavioral theory alienating, overly deterministic, and incongruent with my belief in free will and my understanding of human agency. Later on, I studied constructivism, which made intuitive sense, yet in its application within developmentally appropriate practice (Bredekamp, 1987) seemed to gloss over the differences between children in favor of fairly limiting and prescriptive age-defined guidelines for instruction. From my perspective as a curriculum theorist, neither behavioral nor constructivist theory addressed curricular decision making except by implication. Rather, each theory had generated a system of pedagogical practice that seemed to deny the existence of distinctive curricular issues.

In retrospect, the path by which I reached these beliefs is traceable, at least to me. As an educator, my continuing focus has been on improving the lives of children. I recognize, however, that my interest in issues of diversity, privilege, and equity began much earlier. Thus, I have constructed an autobiographical analysis of how my commitment to social justice came to be integral to my personal identity and my life's work.

Interdependence

Several incidents during my childhood contributed to my emerging concerns with issues of privilege, of self-determination, of interdependence, and so forth. I grew up in Glen Flora, a small, rural village in the northwestern part of Wisconsin. My father worked in a lumberyard, and my mother taught elementary school. As preschoolers, my sisters and I often stayed on the farm with our grandparents during the week and came home for weekends. Family members were everywhere, and my cousins were my closest playmates. Our local extended family included two sets of grandparents and many aunts, uncles, and cousins scattered through out our village and the surrounding township. Help for harvesting crops or building outbuildings was readily available, and the elderly and sick were cared for by family members along with the children. Walking home from school inevitably meant stopping for candy at the store where my grandfather sometimes worked, visiting my father at the feedmill, or waving to a great aunt as we walked past her house. Clearly, the 1950s nuclear family was not normal for me. I grew up assuming that interdependence and extended families were the norm.

Service

Religious service had been a dominant part of our collective family identity in past generations. My great-grandmother Emma Olson emigrated from Sweden in the mid-1800s as a Baptist missionary. Continuing the family religious vocation, my grandfather, in addition to being a farmer and sometimes general store clerk, also served as a lay preacher in an isolated neighboring community. Several of my great uncles and their families were missionaries, and I recall, as a child, special church services and family dinners with stories and pictures of their missionary work in China and Africa. I envied the opportunities those distant cousins had to live in such remote and exotic places. When we sang the Sunday School song, "Jesus loves the little children, all the children in the world," I had no doubt as to equal inclusion of all peoples in this vision of heavenly peace. Raised within an ethic of a universal love for all people, I learned to value difference and equality as essential parts of human life. Later, even while confronting the colonizing nature of my ancestors' missionary work, I held on to the conviction that their efforts extended from a real commitment to helping others, and I sought that commitment for myself as well.

Privilege

My childhood seemed ordinary. We lived on the edge of town, and I was free to roam the countryside, the big sister taking care of younger sisters and cousins. My normal school-trained teachers, no doubt influenced by the ideas of John Dewey and William Kilpatrick, planned lessons around the project method and espoused the ideals of democracy, even while presenting us with a white-washed curriculum. We built twig forts, learned Central American songs and dances, and went on field trips to sketch trees and streams. In the summer we picked beans alongside migrant workers to earn money for school clothes. As a community we were rural, poor, and relatively isolated from mainstream American culture. In 1960, we counted only two televisions in the households of my 20-some classmates—and only three families had flush toilets. The family of one of my best friends still got their water from a pump and heated the main rooms of their house with a wood-burning stove. With no movie theaters in our village and limited access to automobiles, our adolescent world included local school activities, ice skating, deer shining, and occasional multigenerational parties at someone's house.

It was only when I first went to the University of Wisconsin in Madison as an undergraduate student that I realized that my life in Rusk County was far different from that of most of my peers. Difference took on a whole new meaning for me as I recognized that not everyone had the same experiences or opportunities. I took my "cultural deprivation" seriously and began to tutor myself in art, music, and literature. At the same time, I began volunteer work with the local Head Start agency and also at a community center on the west side of Chicago. I was determined that I would make a difference in children's lives, that others would have the opportunities that I missed.

Relevance

After graduation, I began my teaching career in a small southern Wisconsin city not far from Madison. During the day, I taught literature and composition in high school, and two evenings each week I tutored Chicano/a workers at a nearby migrant camp. Although I enjoyed working with the teenagers during the day, I felt much more effective at the camp—relying on the bond of our shared experience as field workers to break the language barrier. I was puzzled that my "remedial" sophomore English class hated Macbeth so intensely and that, after teaching the play, I also began to dislike it. I did not understand why the chairman of the English department criticized my playing a record of Simon and Garfunkel's popular song, "I am a rock—I am an island . . . and a rock feels no pain and an island never cries," to help these same students understand John Donne's "Meditation 17, No Man Is an Island." Believing that the problem was one of my inadequate understanding of adolescent development and teaching strategies, I quit my job at the end of the school year and went back to the University for graduate study, leaving behind the high school students and Chicano/a families with whom I had built connections.

I returned to the public schools 2 years later to work in another small rural district as a school psychologist. Although I was no longer an English teacher, I recognized the same issues from my earlier teaching experience. I questioned why the self-contained classrooms for the mentally retarded had so many bright and verbal Chicano/a children in them and I became involved in an intensive assessment program to re-place these children in regular classrooms. I began to see more clearly the connection between children's experiences, their language, and the curriculum. I also joined the elementary staff in their curriculum-planning meetings and began to consider the possibilities of integrated curriculum and child-centered education.

As my interest in younger children grew, I volunteered to teach summer school in a reading enrichment program for migrant children in the community. Once again, I saw the formal curriculum fail to engage the children with whom I worked. I began organizing field trips around our community and discovered that the stories we wrote about our personal, everyday experiences—the fishing expeditions, trips to the beach, and playground picnic—were much more relevant and effective reading materials for the migrant children than the SRA reading kits the district had provided.

The pattern of these experiences became obvious. I began to think more critically about what I knew about child development and diversity and about how the instructional materials, basal readers, and teaching strategies used in classrooms did not relate to, in any way, the life experiences of the poor, rural, and migrant children with whom I worked. Unfortunately, just as my colleagues and I had identified ourselves as a core staff committed to transforming elementary education, an administrative realignment forced programmatic changes, including the return to a more "basic" curriculum. Once again, I reluctantly left the "kids" behind and moved on, wondering why my educational philosophy never seemed to "fit in" with the school systems in which I worked.

Self-Determination

I spent the next 4 years supervising student teachers and working with the Rock County Head Start Program. I discovered, for the first time, that I could initiate changes to address the many difficulties the families in our program were encountering. We created a home-based model to serve rural and remote families, supported parents in completing their GEDs, and provided child development associate (CDA) training for staff. I became frustrated, however, when I could not find a way to raise staff salaries above the poverty level or eliminate their dependence on welfare in the summer when the program did not operate. How, I asked, could we help families to become economically self-sufficient when, as teachers, we were not able to achieve that for ourselves?

After several years of struggling to support my own children on the meager salary I earned with Head Start, I returned to Madison and university life. The summer of 1976 was a critical period of intellectual and personal transition for me. Michael Apple's seminar on elementary curriculum introduced me to the notion of "hidden curriculum," which I immediately recognized as providing a framework to account for many of the problems I had observed in schools. I looked back at my experiences with Macbeth and my high school sophomores; at the white houses with picket fences in the basal readers provided to the migrant students who lived in field shanties; and at the Alpha–Time letter puppets and Peabody Kit circus posters for the 4-year-old children in Head Start classrooms who had never been to a supermarket or ridden an elevator. Reflecting on the developmental and cultural differences among the children with whom I worked and the inequitable distribution of resources across their lives, I became convinced that change was essential.

A second experience that summer helped put what I was learning into a new perspective. George, an African American policeman and the partner of a colleague, Mary, shot himself through the head in Mary's bathroom. He had just been served with papers for nonsupport of his former wife and children and could not, according to Mary, stand the humiliation of being taken to court and possibly jailed. In completing a journal assignment for a graduate seminar, I wrote about George's life and connected it to T.S. Eliot's "Love Song of J. Alfred Prufrock," focusing on how George had found himself "pinned and wiggling on the wall," trying to deal with the futility and shame he was experiencing. "All of these things I'm learning," I wrote, "what do they have to do with George and Mary and her kids, and with me and my kids, too?"

Alienation

Graduate school had become a blur: classes, a day job at the University, evening teaching in the local technical college in a day-care apprenticeship program, two children to support. I began reading poetry, autobiography, and novels again: Doris Lessing, Nadine Gordimer, Marge Piercy, Adrienne Rich, May Sarton, and later Margaret Atwood. Their stories spoke to my experience in a way that traditional educational texts never had. I began to look at my work through my life experience as a woman. Reading, I identified my alienation from the elite, male world of the University and my reality as an outsider in academe. Recognizing that I was still, at heart, a rural working-class woman, I dropped to part-time status as a doctoral student and accepted a teaching position at a local college, hoping to regain balance in my life.

My subsequent academic positions occasionally have provided me with a haven from which to reflect upon where I have been and what I want to do. At Edgewood College, where I taught for 7 years, the Dominican nuns shared my social commitment and supported me in integrating the campus preschool with Head Start children and in starting a campus day-care center for faculty and students. At the University of Oregon, I joined colleagues who were fully committed to social justice and multicultural education, only to have our program in culture, language, and diversity eliminated. And since that time, my work in reconceptualizing early childhood education has brought me together with a large and diverse group of scholars who share my commitment to social justice and who recognize the social and cultural valuing inherent in our decision making around what knowledge is of most worth for young children.

Reconceptualization

I have come to share the social constructionist theory that children regularly interpret and make sense of their own worlds and that learning can be understood only from the subjective point of view of the participants within their own cultural and interactional contexts. I recognize that, just as I have done in this narrative, we all bring our own experiences as children to our understandings of childhood and that our various social constructions of the young child may constrain our understandings of what children are actually able to learn or of what meanings their activities may have for them. I now recognize more clearly that my personal understanding of childhood, emanating as it does from my rural midwestern cultural experience, also imposes both limitations and expectations on my thinking about children and curriculum—often making me complicit in the reproduction of my own version of dominant European American thinking.

Finally, I have identified two current raging issues for the reconceptualist community:

1. *The relationships of theory, research, and practice.* This debate has ensued across multiple sites—access to reconceptualist work for local early childhood practitioners, opportunities to enhance participant understanding, creation of a space for theoretically driven reconceptualizations, and examination of language usage and the privileging of certain theoretically com-

plex and often obtuse forms of discourse—with the central issue seeming to be often-conflicting desires to stay practically grounded while exploring theoretical questions at the margins of early childhood and beyond.

2. *Understandings of multiplicity and subjectivity.* This discussion alternately has engaged considerations of the dualisms seemingly inherent in talking about topics such as developmentally appropriate practice or cultural diversity; the disputed role of the expert, or researcher, or early childhood professional in working with children and families; or the very existence of reconceptualization as an issue for the field and its elasticity in responding to the needs, interests, and perspectives of interested participants—all seeming to circle around the positioning we assume relative to one another and our work.

One last thought—increasingly I have found myself drifting away from the field of early childhood into other arenas where my questions and interests seem more compatible. The reconceptualizing movement has become my tie to early childhood education, pulling me insistently, gently back. For that I am glad.

HEAD START COMMUNITIES OF LEARNERS: AN EMERGING AGENDA FOR INQUIRY AND PRAXIS

By Rebecca Kantor & David E. Fernie

As we write this essay, we are experiencing the distinctive excitement of taking our perspective (a sociocultural one) to a new "problem," the eager anticipation of working with new colleagues, and the unusual feeling (both luxury and burden) of being sponsored by a new and substantial federal grant. With our colleagues James Scott, Chuck Lynd, and Dennis Sykes, we recently received a grant from the U.S. Department of Education to prepare "technology-proficient teachers for tomorrow": very modernist terms indeed—technology, proficiency, tomorrow. We were able to persuade our funders that early childhood teachers, in particular Head Start teachers, deserved a place in the federal project, although it was originally intended for preservice, grades K–12 teacher education programs. Essentially, we proposed in our grant application to disperse the majority of the money we received to support the creation of 12 local communities of learners (in Indiana, Illinois, and Ohio), with Head Start teachers as the core participants.

The rest of the money will be used to support an infrastructure of both technological and human resources that will be available to all of these communities of learners. Based on our design, Head Start grantees will initiate these "communities" and will seek participants from local 2- and 4-year higher education faculty and their early childhood/elementary preservice students, and from staff and parents involved in local community computer centers, local family literacy programs, and child-care centers.

The Department of Education's goals are to fund innovative preservice programs in order to create technology-proficient teachers for elementary schools within low-income communities; we argued that Head Start teachers already work in such communities, are typically involved in preservice programs in response to the recent federal mandate to further their education by the year 2003, and thus provide a natural, situated, alternative pathway leading (some) to degrees that will allow them to teach in the elementary schools of their communities.

From our current sociocultural perspective, we believe that a strong social group will be an essential vehicle for the accomplishment of all of these goals. This is because of the inherent strengths in a social construction process: dialogue among participants with multiple perspectives; social support (crucial for nontraditional students); and situated, "close to the action" instruction and exploration of both curricular and professional development issues (as opposed to the traditional separation between practice and higher education experiences, particularly at 4-year institutions). Technological proficiency, we hope, will be the natural outcome of using technology to communicate—participants will use e-mail, videoconferencing, and Internet bulletin boards, and will engage in distance education experiences such as web-based coursework—all useful tools to make credit-bearing college experiences more accessible and interactive. In addition, we hope that participants' use of technology to support meaningful learning experiences will create a disposition toward technology use that also will spread to their work with children.

As a part of this new project, we have a similar interest in creating a strong social group to support the research that we will conduct with the participants in the communities of learners. Out of ongoing dialogue at the Reconceptualizing Early Childhood Education meetings, and in other contexts, a group of researchers across three American states, Sweden, and Australia, all with teacher education projects and broadly shared assumptions and values, have come together to create a community of researchers, a social group to support our collective work in our respective settings. Again, we anticipate the inherent strengths of a social construction process: dialogue across multiple perspectives, critique and sharing of expertise, and social support. Similar to the communities of learners project, we will use a combination of face-to-face interaction and virtual contexts for interaction (e.g., web-based text sharing, desktop videoconferencing, and e-mail). We are interested in exploring different cross-setting and cross-cultural cases of how people form supportive contexts for the professional development of nontraditional teachers, and how researchers and teacher educators can both facilitate and reveal such processes.

How did these new goals and reconceptualized ways of working with people evolve for us over time? Briefly, the essential impetus for this transition was to find a better match between the nature of our "burning" questions and the lens to explore them. Child development theory does not provide us with a way to understand the social construction of everyday life and how the early childhood educational and social processes of interest to us—play, friendship, peer culture, language and literacy, participation in school culture—are situated within this group life. In a long-term, ethnographic study within a single preschool classroom, we explored many of these topics with our colleagues through a series of linked and mutually informing sociocultural analyses. One of the distinctive aspects of this project was our ability to work very close to the action of this classroom, blurring the usual insider/outsider dichotomy by having several adult participants engaged in both the classroom teaching and the research. What emerged during this overtime experience was the satisfaction of working collaboratively with graduate students and a strong collaborative partnership with each other that has survived the tensions of tenure and promotion review at a large research university with the individualistic and positivistic traditions of the academy. So within our research we reconceptualized the theoretical perspective guiding our work, the social structure formed to conduct that research, and our faculty roles across two colleges, at a time when we had to be concerned with conservative traditions of university cultures.

As we moved forward with this newly constructed approach, we nevertheless discovered the value in deconstructing this experience as well. Our work in the preschool ethnography was grounded in the discipline of cognitive anthropology and strongly influenced by the work of our mentors Bill Corsaro and Judith Green. As we encountered the community of early childhood "reconceptualists" and interacted with its members, we benefited from the ongoing dialogue and critique that situate our theoretical perspective among diverse and current critical and postmodern perspectives. This has allowed us to better understand both the benefits and limitations of any single theoretical approach, and has provided a push toward reflection and circumspection. For example, we have long been describing teacher–child interaction, but we now must ask ourselves: How can we describe these interactions without considering issues of power and control? While earlier we might have studied gender as a separate topic, feminist researchers have shown us that most experiences in daily life are gendered. While studying the local culture constructed in the classroom remains for us a valid and important focus of study, we also believe that researchers should not investigate classroom life without an awareness of how wider layers of community and culture are a part of what defines it. We believe that the ultimate impact of ongoing deconstructive and dialogic exchange with colleagues has been to strengthen the theory and broaden the purview of our work, rather than to detract from or diminish its value.

Over the same period of time that we have been in conversation with the reconceptualists, we also have been exploring the work of the educators in Reggio Emilia, Italy (as have a good number of American colleagues). This, too, has helped us to reconceptualize our current agenda. Partly by looking into "the mirror" of another culture, we have been prompted to re-examine our existing frameworks for practice and to identify new educational possibilities as well. In particular, the Italians' practices concerning teacher education are so different from traditional programs of teacher education in the United States that they challenge to us to rethink, at a fundamental level, how we go about preparing educators. In the United States, teachers are educated primarily at the university before employment in schools, while in Reggio Emilia, employment signals the beginning of an ongoing mentoring that takes place in the schools. In the United States, higher education faculty are primarily responsible for the preparation of new teachers (with support from classroom teachers), while in Reggio Emilia, teachers' professional development is the more collective responsibility of peers, *pedagogisti* (roughly equivalent to curriculum coordinators), and even parents, rather than higher education faculty. So, traditional teacher education in the United States is more linear and hierarchical, a presocialization with an emphasis on readiness to teach. In Reggio Emilia, teacher education is more situated in practice and more collective, and involves a more on-line enculturation into the life of the classroom, school, and community.

How, then, are the influences of our reconceptualist and Reggio Emilia colleagues and their ideas reflected in our current agenda and our hopes for our work with the Head Start communities of learners? First, the valuing of multiple perspectives is reflected in our consideration of who might participate in these communities of learners. By involving teachers, parents, faculty, administrators, and community program staff, we envision contexts in which diverse perspectives will be held, shared, and considered for the common good. In our community of researchers, too, we seek a similar richness to flow from the fact that the members of the group will bring diverse yet essentially compatible theoretical perspectives, along with expertise and experiences reflecting their diverse cultural contexts. Second, aware of the need to reduce the social hierarchies that often operate in traditional teacher education paradigms, we have self-consciously located our communities of learners close to the action of their practice, and we will encourage each group to develop a collaborative vision of how they will operate. Third, our experiences with our colleagues have provoked us generally to be more experimental in our consideration of the content and conduct of teacher education programs and to place more confidence in the ability of participants to chart many of their own directions. Fourth, these experiences have provoked us to make issues of race, gender, and social class an explicit part of the teacher education agenda for the communities of learners, recognizing their inevitable salience and importance in the fabric of human social interactions.

Finally, we see this project as an opportunity to explore the relationship between inquiry and praxis. Recent discussion among the reconceptualists at AERA and elsewhere has highlighted some participants' desire to be more action/advocacy-oriented in their work—to use research as a tool to improve the lives of communities and to promote social justice. It is our hope (and time will tell) that the work in Head Start communities related to this grant will provide just such an opportunity to promote these wider goals.

TRAVERSING NEW EARLY CHILDHOOD LANDSCAPES

By Richard Johnson

In the past few weeks I've heard some peculiar stories from several people concerning the reconceptualist movement. In one account I was told that a just-hired assistant professor was informed by her senior professors to stay well clear of the reconceptualist movement as it would not help advance her career and her affiliation with the movement actually might hurt her career. In another university a different senior faculty member informed a junior colleague that for all intents and purposes the reconceptualist movement "didn't work, nobody is interested in it any more, and it is dead." Dead? I didn't even know it began!

I'm particularly interested in this notion of "nobody is interested in it," as much of my recent work is in an area of early childhood that nobody seems interested in, namely, *sexuality*. In recent theoretical reviews I had a great deal of difficulty finding the topic "sexuality" in any of the popular early childhood discourse. The sexuality content I did find mentioned in popular texts was dominated by traditional notions that treat sexuality as a simple, unifying, conservative theme. As taught in our classes, sexuality in early childhood education is all about normalcy and safety. Indeed, these are the thematic issues strictly adhered to throughout popular narratives in the field of early education. The field of early education at-large continues valorizing conservative, singular, humanistic perspectives on children and their sexual/developmental progression (i.e., child development as staged-based, universal phenomena; normal behavior; child as innocent), while other more radical perspectives remain mostly silenced. This is at a distinctive time when sexuality has shifted from the margins to the center in many disciplines highly familiar and interrelated to our own work. At a time when we should be enlarging the spaces in which intellectual deliberations about sexuality can be heard, we instead have reduced the dialogue on sexuality.

I want to be involved in intellectual movements that enlarge spaces for critical deliberation, as that process allows for the making of possibilities. The acts of moving out of silence and moving away from ignorance, are what enthuse me most about the reconceptualist movement. This reconceptualist movement revels in the notion of possibility making. Just as my opening paragraph reveals, skeptics continue to claim that this movement is elitist and the theory too difficult and distant from the common practitioner. I disagree with these colonial claims that continue to privilege those skeptics who already know and teach their own uncontested versions of the truth and don't seem willing to be involved in the reconceptualists' "rigorous questioning of the will to truth" (Popkewitz & Brennan, 1998, p. 30). Like Popkewitz and Brennan (1998) and other reconceptualists, I find it liberating to "disrupt how we 'tell the truth' about ourselves and others" (p. 29). This movement is all about making and remaking theory and practice. The reconceptualist movement has been highly successful in assisting me to recognize my own personal and theoretical ignorance. I've witnessed and self-critiqued my own narrow-minded approaches to the field and to the world. With the reconceptualist movement, I've learned to realize how little I questioned during my undergraduate and graduate education and the early part of my academic career. Opposed to my earlier safe theoretical stance(s) on all early childhood truth, I now find myself constantly in shifting states of contestation as I personally and professionally refuse to sit still and participate in the normalization of myself, the field, and the children and families we all study and critique. Borrowing from geography, instead, I'm choosing a variety of theoretical trajectories that I think can assist me in (re)reading the early childhood landscape. I'm interested in theorizing beyond the present conservative, normative theoretical limitations of early childhood education, attempting to think and write well beyond the current stasis in the field as I (re)consider the field more in terms of "space as spaciousness, as the unbounded, the area of total possibility" (Lewis, 1955, cited in Jarvis, 1998).

The reconceptualist movement has helped me actively search for opportunities to cross theoretical and disciplinary borders, made me more politically aware as I move out of the weight of a heavy multiple inheritance (developmental psychology, Piaget, developmentally appropriate practice, and so forth) and attempt to remake myself (Chambers, 1994).

CONFIRMING MULTIPLE VOICES

As we read the voices of colleagues, the experiences that we have shared as educators and our life concerns as human beings emerge. The ever-present concern for those who are younger is obvious in Jan Jipson's title, "All the Children in the World," in Rebecca Kantor and David Fernie's quest to collaborate with the communities that influence children, in Amos Hatch's understanding that picking up a tiny, African American girl changed his life, and in Richard Johnson's concern for the denial of the sexuality of young children. Further, the belief in and celebration of diversity and possibility have led our colleagues to value multiple perspectives and to revise the theoretical vantage points from which they construct their work. Personal experiences with family, professors, and new ideas have influenced everyone. Finally, both optimism and frustration are obvious—optimism for the possibilities to come from diverse viewpoints, recognition of the political, and collaboration; frustration with narrow, dominant, often unconscious ways of limiting those possibilities.

Perhaps more important, these personal/professional stories represent just a few of the multiple voices and identities possible in our field. Jan demonstrates the ways in which reconceptualization is deeply embedded in her entire life through such experiences as the interdependence of her early years, the personal call to service, the lived experience that unmasks privilege, and the alienation of graduate school for a rural working-class woman. While playing an active role in the paradigm wars of the 1980s and 1990s and accepting the challenge to examine taken-for-granted ideas, Amos illustrates his belief in being a "mediator between the mainstream and my 'radical' friends," in asking if discourses are leading to "positive changes for children." Rebecca and David have reconceptualized their work by attempting to reduce hierarchical social structures; integrating issues of power, control, and societal embeddedness (e.g., gendering in society); and generally constructing a disposition of exploration and critique even as they have had to work within conservative traditions. Finally, Richard has very directly taken on a reconceptualist position by addressing the discourses that would disqualify postmodernist possibilities, emphasizing that perhaps in our quests for normalcy and safety, we do not actually respect diversity and possibility. All of the multiple and changing identities explored by these colleagues (with their concerns, issues, ideas, and voices) provide directions for exploration and expanded opportunities for those who are younger.

In the end, we believe that our diverse voices and ways of viewing the world position us for new beginnings. Further, we invite you to engage in your own personal/professional life story as you consider the reconceptualist possibilities offered by the authors of this book.

REFERENCES

Bredekamp, S. (1987). *Developmentally appropriate practice in early childhood programs serving children from birth through age 8*. Washington, DC: National Association for the Education of Young Children.

Chambers, I. (1994). *Migrancy, culture, identity*. New York: Routledge.

de Lone, R. H. (1979). *Small futures*. New York: Harcourt Brace Jovanovich.

Jarvis, B. (1998). *Postmodern cartographies*. New York: St. Martin's Press.

Jipson, J., & Johnson, R. (Eds.). (2000). *Resistance and representation: Rethinking childhood*. New York: Peter Lang.

Popkewitz, T., & Brennan, M. (1998). Restructuring of social and political theory in education: Foucault and a social epistemology of school practices. In T. Popkewitz & M. Brennan (Eds.), *Foucault's challenge: Discourse, knowledge, and power in education* (pp. 3–35). New York: Teachers College Press.

PART II

Counter Identities: Constructions That Limit Education

CHAPTER 3

Miss Nelson Is Missing! Teacher Sightings in Research on Teaching

Sharon Ryan, Mindy Ochsner, & Celia Genishi

The kids in Room 207 were misbehaving again . . .
Now settle down, said Miss Nelson in a sweet voice.
But the class would not settle down . . .
"Something will have to be done," said Miss Nelson.
The next morning Miss Nelson did not come to school.
"Wow! . . . Today let's be just terrible!" they [the students] said.
"Not so fast!" hissed an unpleasant voice . . . "I am your new teacher, Miss Viola Swamp." And she rapped the desk with her ruler . . .
She meant business. Right away she put them to work. And she loaded them down with homework. "We'll have no story hour today," said Miss Swamp. "Keep your mouths shut," said Miss Swamp. "Sit perfectly still," said Miss Swamp. "And if you misbehave, you'll be sorry," said Miss Swamp.
                    —Harry Allard & James Marshall, *Miss Nelson Is Missing!*

IN THE BOOK Miss Nelson Is Missing! (Allard & Marshall, 1977), the children of Room 207 are confronted with a dilemma. In response to their misbehavior, Miss Nelson has taken an unprecedented leave of absence and in her place has emerged Miss Viola Swamp. In many ways Miss Swamp is the antithesis of Miss Nelson.

A feminine teacher, Miss Nelson is drawn with a perfect blonde hair-style, lipsticked smile, attired in a conservative pink dress, and wearing a necklace of pearls with matching earrings. She is young, nice, nurturing, and kind to her students. No matter how rude or inconsiderate her class might be, she is sensitive to their emotional needs and politely asks students to settle down. On the other hand, Miss Viola Swamp is old, autocratic, and simply wretched. She stands before the students, wearing an ugly black dress, her black wiry hair a mess, and she raps on a student's desk with a ruler to gain control of the class. She tells the class what to do and how to do it. She is certainly not tolerant of any infractions of her rules. If Room 207 thought Miss Nelson was a bad teacher, their images are shattered when they have to endure the cruel and intolerant Miss Swamp!

Although they may be characters in a children's story, Miss Nelson and Miss Swamp represent two dominant images of teachers that pervade early childhood (EC) literature, popular culture, and our social imaginations. This dichotomy is represented in the EC literature by the categories of developmentally appropriate or developmentally inappropriate practices (e.g., Bredekamp & Copple, 1997; Schweinhart & Weikhart, 1997). Good EC teachers are those like Miss Nelson, supportive and sensitive educators who, unlike Miss Swamp, are willing to share authority for the learning process with their students.

Our aim in this chapter is to problematize these dominant representations of teaching and EC teachers. We ask, Is it possible to be something other than a Miss Nelson or a Miss Swamp? Can and do teachers incorporate elements of both aspects of these images into their practice of educating young children? In other words, we are interested in what is lost or missing if EC teachers are seen only as *either* developmentally appropriate *or* developmentally inappropriate, as *either* a Miss Nelson *or* a Miss Swamp. To answer these questions, we probe one of the primary producers of images of teachers, research on teaching. Specifically, we look at one historically prevalent program of research on teaching, process–product studies, and juxtapose the images constituted within these texts with those being produced by more contemporary, and some would say more marginalized, approaches to the study of teaching—poststructural studies of early childhood education (ECE). By exploring research on teaching at both the center and margins, we aim to illustrate the possibilities and limitations of different approaches to EC research on teaching and what is suggested both for a new research agenda in ECE and for reconceptualizing the knowledge base of teacher education.

PROCESS–PRODUCT RESEARCH ON TEACHING

Research on teaching usually refers to the large and diverse group of inquiries that explore any activity involving teaching and teachers (Shulman, 1986). In the field of ECE, research on teaching is unique in that historically researchers have focused predominantly on children's learning and development and little on teachers, teaching, or its effects. However, in a recent review of research on teaching in ECE (Genishi, Ryan, Ochsner, & Yarnall, in press), it is evident that the number of studies inquiring into EC teachers and teaching is on the increase. Five differing orientations to the study of EC teaching are outlined in this review—process–product, teacher cognition, ecological studies, teacher research, and critical studies in ECE. Of all these orientations, process–product is the most enduring program of inquiry.

Process–product research seeks to "define the relationships between what teachers do in the classroom (the process of teaching) and what happens to their students (the products of learning)" (Anderson, Evertson, & Brophy, 1979, p. 193). Framed by a positivistic view of science, researchers working in this tradition assume that social processes like teaching and learning are governed by laws similar to those found in nature (Popkewitz, 1984). The purpose of research is to identify the teaching behaviors or general rules of teaching that result in improved student learning and achievement.

In order to ascertain these laws of teaching, process–product researchers model their methods of inquiry on the natural sciences. Knowledge is assumed to be what is observable or based on empirical facts (Popkewitz, 1984). Teaching and learning are studied as behaviors free of context and the varying meanings and values individuals bring to the research situation (Lubeck, 1998). In order to conduct objective scientific inquiries that will elicit accurate accounts of teaching, process–product researchers employ a range of quantitative techniques and procedures. Viewing the social world as an interacting system of discernible variables, they identify and measure specific teaching behaviors, observing these variables across a number of settings in a random sample of the population so that data can be compared and generalizations about effective teaching drawn.

Process–Product Research in Lower Elementary Grades

What might be considered traditional process–product research studies in EC often are situated in the lower elementary grades and usually focus on the achievement of basic academic skills using student test scores as measures of teacher effectiveness. Morris, Blanton, Blanton, Nowacek, and Perney (1995), for instance, conducted an experimental study in 7 third-grade classrooms to investigate the effects of adapting instructional materials to meet the needs of low-achieving spellers.

After identifying 48 low-achieving spellers in these classrooms, the researchers divided the group in half. Twenty-four children in four of the classes were designated as the intervention group and received instruction from a second-grade spelling book. The remaining 24 children in the three other classes were used as the control and comparison group. Spelling lessons were observed for each teacher over a week in the fall and a week in the spring during which written and audiotaped observations were recorded.

When all seven teachers were observed teaching their whole class, instruction was found to be similar—they introduced the spelling words on the first day of the week, guided students through spelling book practice activities for most of the week, and gave a spelling test on Friday. The four intervention teachers did not always teach in a whole-group manner, however, but chose to group students by ability in spelling—teaching third-grade-level words to the high-ability group, while the low achievers were taught second-grade words. Using similar techniques to teach spelling to each ability group as to teach the whole class, the intervention teachers altered the instructional time spent with each group of students and the kinds of tests and activities they assigned. Once the words and practice activities had been introduced to children at the beginning of the week, the high-ability students were expected to complete a series of spelling book activities independently, while the teacher helped the students in the low-ability group with their second-grade spelling activities. On Fridays, second-grade tests were given to the low-achieving group, and third-grade tests were given to the high-achieving group.

To determine how effective individualized instruction with lower-grade spelling materials was for students struggling in spelling, every student was pre- and posttested on the same curriculum-based spelling tests for both second and third grades. On the pretest, no significant differences were found between low-achieving spellers. On the posttest, however, those low-achieving students who had received instruction from the second-grade book outperformed the comparison group on the second-grade spelling posttest. No significant difference was found between the two groups on the third-grade spelling posttest. Despite concerns of several of the intervention teachers about teaching their low-achieving, third-grade students with materials below grade level, Morris and colleagues (1995) argue that these findings demonstrate the importance of teaching children at a level where they can experience success.

Morris and colleagues (1995) measured the success of using second-grade spelling books to meet the needs of low-achieving spellers simply and conclusively by comparing children's test scores before and after some of them received a planned intervention. When examining teaching in the years before school, however, determining the effects of different strategies becomes more complicated. There is a unique distinction between process–product studies in the early elementary years of school compared with studies conducted of teaching in child-care, family day-care, and preschool settings. We call the latter studies process–process, in that the outcomes for students become different kinds of process-based behaviors, like problem solving, play preferences, and social competence, while the processes of teaching become more concerned with the emotional and nurturing characteristics of teachers. In exploring the effects of teacher practices, these studies highlight the field's particular concerns with child development, rather than student achievement in academic subjects (Goffin, 1989).

Process–Process Research in Early Childhood Education

An exemplar of process–process research is a longitudinal study conducted by Howes (1997) to examine the relationships among caregiver sensitivity, children's attachment security, and their social competence with peers. The teachers in this study were the primary caregivers working with 107 children in licensed family day-care homes and one child-care center. Observations were conducted on the interactions between these caregivers and the focal children on two separate occasions.

During these two observation periods, adult sensitivity to children was measured using the Arnett (1989) rating scale for caregiver sensitivity. A caregiver was rated as sensitive if she or he encouraged a child to try new experiences, harsh if she or he were unnecessarily rough when scolding or prohibiting children, and detached if she or he spent considerable time in an activity not involving interaction with the children. At the end of each observation of several hours, the Attachment Q-set was used to rate children's attachment relationships with their teachers. Additionally, children's play was rated on a peer play scale ranging from solitary play and low-level play behavior to complementary-reciprocal play.

From these various measures, Howes (1997) found that with more time in child care, children tended to become secure and engaged in higher-level forms of social play with their peers. Similarly, over time the children's caregivers were observed to become more sensitive to the children in their care. When the relations among security, caregiving behaviors, and peer play were examined, it also was found that the more children received sensitive caregiving, the more secure they were and the more they engaged in complex peer play.

According to these findings, Howes (1997) concludes that caregivers do influence children's play with their peers. However, because the levels of children's social play were found to correlate with the amount of time spent in child care, Howes argues that this relationship is an indirect one. Young children construct more complex interactions with their peers over time, but sensitive caregivers provide the necessary support that enables young children to independently establish relationships with other children.

Dominant Teaching Images

The different foci of process–product and process–process studies elicit different but dominant images of early childhood teachers. In the study by Morris and colleagues (1995), teaching is portrayed in a manner similar to the style of Miss Swamp. Just as Miss Swamp employs firm and clear disciplinary strategies that get particular results from her children, teaching in the Morris and colleagues study also is represented as a top-down and technical process. Ensuring the academic success of low-achieving spellers is as simple as varying the materials used to teach these students. These teachers are seen by the researchers not as professionals, but as technicians who improve their teaching because they have been trained to individualize the commercial materials they use to teach spelling.

Alternatively, because teachers are rated according to their levels of sensitivity to young children, the image of early childhood teachers in the Howes (1997) study is more akin to Miss Nelson. Sensitive caregivers are responsive to young children's needs. They encourage children to try new experiences, provide safe environments, and give emotional support as needed. However, despite less oppressive images of early childhood teachers, Howes also gives little recognition to the kinds of intellectual work required on the part of teachers who work with very young children in child care. Sensitive caregivers are those who facilitate children's development by being warm and caring, but they do not necessarily reflect on their interactions and practices.

Regardless of these differing images, the emphasis on empirical-analytic techniques that reduce teaching to observable and measurable behaviors limits the representations of EC teachers and teaching produced by process–product and process–process studies. Teachers in these studies are represented not as thoughtful individuals with biographies, but as a set of limited teaching behaviors described in relation to an instructional strategy, a child outcome, or a specific program model. Markers of identity such as gender, class, sexuality, and cultural background are not considered relevant to understanding what teachers do in their classrooms. In the quest to be objective and scientific, teachers allow the multiple roles and identities they take on and the range of strategies they employ in a particular context to be subsumed by a set of methods (Britzman, 1991) or interactional characteristics. Ignoring the interplay of context, biography, and values in the shaping of teaching practices leads to an oversimplified account of what it means to be a teacher of young children.

POSTSTRUCTURAL STUDIES OF TEACHING

When the methodological and epistemological lenses used by researchers shift from modern values of certain and generalizable truths about teaching to a postmodern focus on the local and dynamic aspects of teaching, more complex images of EC teachers are possible. One set of theories that embrace these postmodern values in their explorations of social life are labeled poststructuralist.

Poststructuralism is an umbrella term employed to define a diverse array of approaches concerned with the politics of knowledge and educational practices (Anyon, 1994; Tobin, 1995). For poststructuralists, power is central to all social relations and is expressed and exercised through discourses. Discourses are socially organized frameworks of meaning embodying particular values and practices that stipulate rules and domains of what can be said and done, by whom, and when (Burman, 1994; Hicks, 1995–96). Thus, discourses have a material, social, and linguistic existence and enact particular power effects. "Social processes like teaching and learning therefore cannot be understood without understanding the operation of power in discourses and especially how discourses privilege certain interests within particular societies at specific points in their history" (Mac Naughton, 1994, p. 93).

In their creation of differing relations of power, discourses also produce subjectivity or the ways we come to define ourselves and the authority we feel in particular situations. Individuals take up particular discourses, "speaking and writing them into existence as if they were their own" (Davies, 1993, p. 13). As human beings, we do not reside in one stable discourse but instead we belong to different social groups (e.g., gender, race, class, children, teachers), each group circulating its own discourse and enacting practices that define what it means to be human (Davies, 1990). Because there are multiple discourses circulating in social life, individuals can either take up the subject position offered by a particular discourse or resist the categorizations being assigned to their subjectivity through competing discourses. Thus, poststructuralists assume human subjectivity shifts and changes depending on one's positioning in discourse (Anyon, 1994; Wexler, 1987).

The purpose of poststructural research is not only to provide descriptions of early childhood teaching but to critically examine classroom practices and social relations. Because poststructuralism is a relatively new theoretical lens being applied to research on teaching and a theory that seeks to be antifoundational, there is no one way of doing poststructural research. However, many poststructuralist studies take as their starting point that knowledge is a social construction involving relations of power. The research process itself is viewed as a subjective and biased enterprise that creates a particular politics of knowledge. In order to prevent the research process from marginalizing those who are being researched, dialogic and self-reflexive research designs are advocated (Lather, 1991). Researchers attempt to include participants in the research process, and methods are used to prevent the researcher's theoretical perspective from being the only lens through which data are analyzed and represented.

As poststructuralists assume that there are no universal truths free of human values and interests, qualitative methods usually are employed to gather data on classroom discourses at local sites of practice. Analysis does not focus solely on patterns of interaction but examines the contradictions and inconsistencies observed in classroom relations. In making sense of how discourses in classrooms operate to produce particular meanings and truths, poststructuralists argue that it then becomes possible to insert alternative discourses that might address inequities that exist in the classroom and beyond.

Many researchers working within a poststructural frame for ECE have focused on gendered power relations. Ochsner (1999b), for example, utilizes feminist poststructuralism to illuminate the multiple gender discourses circulating in an urban kindergarten classroom and how they permeate the construction and legitimization of students' gender. As a participant-observer, Ochsner collected data over a 6-month period, taking field notes, audiotaping and videotaping classroom talk and actions, interviewing students and the teacher, and collecting student artifacts.

Although this study focused on how students constructed themselves as gendered beings, Ochsner also documented how the classroom teacher, Isabel, accepted her own power and authority to intentionally create opportunities in the curriculum for students to enact individual agency and consciousness about gender discourses. Isabel often was observed using workshare, a classroom ritual where students' work is highlighted and discussed in a public forum, to bring gender issues to the foreground of the curriculum. Audiotaped transcriptions show Isabel explicitly and consciously coordinating workshare so that students' multiple perspectives about gender were publicly exposed. Not only did Isabel encourage students to talk about their individual understandings about gender, but she also worked dialectically with students, drawing from her own and others' experiences, to further challenge gender norms. By manipulating and orchestrating workshare to include competing, and often biased, understandings about gender, Isabel encouraged students to question and confront narrow assumptions of gender. For Isabel, teaching is a political act, as she explains:

> It's amazing to me that thinking about and talking about something are forms of social action. And what you put out there for them to think about is important, what you put into the center of the culture circle. When you are thinking about something it is action, you're lifting it up to the light. And that's when research and teaching becomes social action. (Ochsner, 1999a, p. 12)

Thus Ochsner's study illuminates the ways in which this teacher purposefully exposed gender discourses in order to interrogate students' sexist understandings of being either a girl or a boy.

In a recent case study of teaching and learning in an urban kindergarten classroom, Ryan (1998) employed poststructural social theory to examine the power relations constituting child-centered education. Concentrating her observations on periods of student choice in the curriculum, Ryan used field notes and audio- and videotaped observations to document the talk and action of the teacher and a select group of children over a 5-month period. Interviews structured around videotaped classroom scenes also were conducted at various points of the study for the purpose of constructing multiple readings of classroom events.

After conducting a critical discourse analysis of the collected data, Ryan found that the teacher, Alison, moved primarily between two discourses that gave shape to her identity and pedagogy as an early childhood educator. The first of these was the developmental discourse, which creates the meanings and practices associated with child-centered education. Alison did not identify herself as a developmentalist, but she drew on developmental theory and the liberal-humanist assumptions that frame those ideas to create a curriculum where children were encouraged to become competent learners (independent, self-motivated, persistent) by having some choice and authority over their learning. Alison structured this sharing of authority into her curriculum by providing a daily choice time and allowing children to suggest activities and themes for curriculum content, while she took on a more facilitative and supportive role in their learning.

Being child-centered for Alison meant starting with children's needs and interests, which necessitated that she also be more direct in her instructional interactions with some children. In order to resist the developmental discourse, which defines good teaching as teaching from behind and therefore positions teachers who choose to enact a more adult-oriented approach as morally incorrect, Alison drew on her experiences working in all-Black schools with African American teachers. In this community, direct and explicit instruction and an emphasis on young children learning academic knowledge are validated as means of ensuring that students are successful in school. Thus Alison often chose to position herself in the urban educational discourse to impose limits on student choice in the curriculum, to use choice time as a play and practice time, and to explicitly evaluate children's productivity. In Alison's words, "I'm going to give you some choices but this is what you're going to do because if you don't you maybe never will" (Ryan, 1998, p. 119).

Alison's movement between these different and contradictory discourses of teaching created tensions in her pedagogy. On some days and in particular social relations Alison sometimes felt she became too much of an authority in children's learning:

> There [are] some times that I don't feel as upset about being as direct. I think sometimes around social things I don't mind being as direct as I do sometimes around content types of things. . . . When it gets to content stuff I definitely am uncomfortable saying "You know I'm going to tell you, now go do it." (p. 132)

At the same time, these contradictory teaching practices also were combined by Alison in unique and innovative ways to provide what she deemed to be a child-centered education.

These poststructural studies of early childhood teachers illustrate that there "is nothing essential about who a teacher is or becomes—it is only through discourses that teachers can be viewed as possessing essential qualities" (Britzman, 1991, p. 223). By assuming that subjectivity is fluid and dynamic, these studies illuminate the ways in which teachers take on multiple subjectivities as they combine different and sometimes what often are assumed to be incompatible practices to interact with young children. Isabel and Alison, for instance, take on identities akin to both Miss Nelson and Miss Swamp, choosing at times to direct children's constructions of the world and at other times to allow children to take more of a lead in their learning. Moreover, by examining teaching as the production of discourses, poststructural studies illuminate the range of knowledges and experiences teachers draw on to exercise power in their worlds. Teachers are portrayed as clever thinkers and actors involved in a complicated web of social relationships that create possibilities as well as constraints for curriculum and pedagogy.

MOVING BEYOND IMAGES OF GOOD VERSUS BAD TEACHERS

Our intent in this chapter has been to probe the images of teachers produced by different programs of research on teaching. In some ways it may seem that we have conducted a relatively simplistic analysis as we have chosen two programs of research that are the antithesis of each other in theoretical and methodological orientation. Moreover, surveying two studies that are deemed "typical" of process–product research obscures the many innovative investigations or hybrid studies that extend this paradigm of inquiry (e.g., Duffy, 1993). Therefore, it is not difficult to argue that the epistemological framework employed by poststructuralists creates more complex images of early childhood teachers and teaching. The most logical next step, then, might be to outline a research agenda that dismisses the efforts of those working in the program of process–product research in favor of inquiries that examine early childhood teaching from a critical-theoretical perspective. Rather than limiting programs of research, however, it is more fruitful to think about how existing programs can be reconceptualized and new programs devised that produce multiple images of early childhood teachers and the complicated task of teaching young children. It is with the aim of framing such a new research agenda and its implications for preparing new teachers that we make the following suggestions.

First, as part of this effort to reconceptualize the knowledge base, it is necessary to rethink research aimed at determining effective teaching. We support the efforts of researchers in the process–product orientation to elucidate the kinds of teaching strategies that enhance student learning. However, we are unconvinced that this can be done within a paradigm that assumes that specified teacher behaviors cause specified learner outcomes. We therefore recommend the contextualizing of "products" so that we understand how they came to be constructed and what they mean for learners and teachers. In this way, it may be possible to construct teachers as thinkers as well as actors in the educative process.

Second, researchers need to devise strategies that limit the distance between themselves and the teachers they study. The poststructural studies reviewed in this chapter go some way toward achieving this aim. However, the theoretical frameworks employed by these researchers, with their opaque language and explicit political purposes, may not always be the lenses teachers choose for judging and explaining their work. Some teachers have argued that they find academic theories deficient in their application to the challenges of classroom life, no matter how complex the theory may claim to be (Genishi, Dubetz, & Focarino, 1995). If we are to construct more diverse images of EC teachers, these differences should not be silenced. Rather, they can be the basis for difficult conversations about the alternative values and visions teachers and researchers bring to their constructions of EC teaching.

Third, the postmodern values embraced by poststructural researchers, among others working from a critical-theoretical orientation (e.g., queer theorists, postcolonial theorists, and some feminists), lead to the deconstruction of either/or dualisms used to limit categorizations of early childhood teachers. However, many of these theoretical frameworks are at the margin, not in the mainstream, of research on teaching and take as their starting point a critique of the traditional early childhood project grounded in psychological theories of development. Clearly, we need an increase in the number of studies utilizing these alternative frameworks if we are to construct more diverse images of EC teachers. Just as important, however, is finding ways to include these research studies and the alternative theories framing them as part of the knowledge base of early childhood teacher education. This will require the forging of alliances across disciplinary boundaries so that we engage in dialogue about our differences and together construct new studies and multiple readings of EC teaching.

Within the EC field, we suggest the inclusion of concrete research activities in teacher education courses that instigate a thoughtful and critical dialogue about prospective or current teachers' images of themselves or their colleagues. For example:

1. Analysis of feature films that portray images of EC teachers, such as *Matilda* and *Kindergarten Cop*, to reveal ways that creators of popular culture view EC teaching
2. Deconstruction of one's drawings of teaching in an EC classroom after reading this chapter to unmask the images represented
3. Critical analysis of pictures, drawings, and/or photographs of teachers represented in EC and elementary professional journals (e.g., *Childhood Education*, *The Reading Teacher*, *Young Children*)

These kinds of activities will involve participants in an action-oriented research process in which they themselves engage in constructing more complex representations of teachers and teaching. Such experiences and the participants' personal practical knowledge (Clandinin, 1985) underlie their own theories, which are situated, relational, and derived from multiple sources (Richardson, 1994). Thus, our fourth recommendation is for academics to conduct more studies with EC teachers and to expand the knowledge base about teaching by including the research of teachers (e.g., Ballenger, 2000; Gallas, 1998; Stires, 1991).

Altering dominant images of EC teachers is a challenging task. To rise to this challenge, teachers, researchers, and theorists will need to work together to co-construct an ongoing agenda for thought and action. Central to this agenda must be the development of knowledge bases and methods of inquiry that grapple with the interplay of biography, context, and identity in relation to what is conceptualized as teaching and research, theory and practice. But perhaps more important, this new research agenda requires scholars to recognize the complexities, inconsistencies, and ever-changing dynamics of teaching and to acknowledge that their methods can never fully categorize, explicate, or elucidate teaching, nor should they. As Alison so articulately puts it:

> Teachers who run very similar classrooms may very well have very different philosophies about why they do what they do. This idea that there is a blind adherence among early childhood teachers to a prescribed pedagogy does not fit with my experience. And, in fact, I find it belittling of the intelligence, the professionalism, and the thoughtfulness of many

early childhood teachers. Most of us freely admit to a certain mosaic quality—depending on the child, the situation, even the time of the day or
time of the year. We do our best to piece it together, hopefully recognizing
the strengths and limitations of different practices as well as the struggles
that these practices might present to the range of children before us.
(Ryan, 1998, pp. 345–346)

REFERENCES

Allard, H., & Marshall, J. (1977). *Miss Nelson is missing!* Boston: Houghton
    Mifflin.
Anderson, L., Evertson, C., & Brophy, J. (1979). An experimental study of ef-
    fective teaching in first-grade reading groups. *Elementary School Journal,
    79,* (4), 193–223.
Anyon, J. (1994). The retreat of Marxism and social feminism: Postmodern and
    post-structural theories in education. *Curriculum Inquiry, 24*(2), 115–133.
Arnett, J. (1989). Caregivers in day care centers: Does training matter? *Journal
    of Applied Developmental Psychology, 10,* 541–552.
Ballenger, C. (2000). *Teaching other people's children: Literacy and learning
    in a bilingual classroom.* New York: Teachers College Press.
Bredekamp, S., & Copple, C. (1997). *Developmentally appropriate practice in early
    childhood programs serving children from birth through age 8* (rev. ed.).
    Washington, DC: National Association for the Education of Young Children.
Britzman, D. P. (1991). *Practice makes practice: A critical study of learning to
    teach.* Albany: State University of New York Press.
Burman, E. (1994). *Deconstructing developmental psychology.* London: Routledge.
Clandinin, J. (1985). Personal practical knowledge: A study of teachers' class-
    room images. *Curriculum Inquiry, 15,* 361–385.
Davies, B. (1990). Agency as a form of discursive practice: A classroom scene
    observed. *British Journal of Sociology of Education, 11*(3), 341–361.
Davies, B. (1993). *Shards of glass: Children reading and writing beyond gen-
    dered identities.* St. Leonards, NSW: Allen & Unwin.
Duffy, G. G. (1993). Rethinking strategy instruction for teachers' development
    and their low achievers' understandings. *Elementary School Journal,
    93*(3), 231–247.
Gallas, K. (1998). *"Sometimes I can be anything": Power, gender, and identity
    in a primary classroom.* New York: Teachers College Press.
Genishi, C., Dubetz, N., & Focarino, C. (1995). Reconceptualizing theory
    through practice: Insights from a first grade teacher and second language
    theorists. In S. Reifel (Ed.), *Advances in early education and day care*
    (Vol. 7, pp. 123–152). Greenwich, CT: JAI Press.
Genishi, C., Ryan, S., Ochsner, M., & Yarnall, M. M. (in press). Teaching in
    early childhood education: Understanding practices through research and
    theory. In V. Richardson (Ed.), *Handbook of research on teaching* (4th
    ed.). Washington, DC: American Educational Research Association.

Goffin, S. G. (1989). Developing a research agenda for early childhood education: What can be learned from research on teaching? *Early Childhood Research Quarterly, 4,* 187–204.

Hicks, D. (1995–96). Discourse, learning, and teaching. In M. Apple (Ed.), *Review of research in education* (No. 21, pp. 49–95). Washington, DC: American Educational Research Association.

Howes, C. (1997). Teacher sensitivity, children's attachment and play with peers. *Early Education and Development, 8*(1), 41–49.

Lather, P. (1991). *Getting smart: Feminist research and pedagogy with/in the postmodern.* New York: Routledge.

Lubeck, S. (1998). Is developmentally appropriate practice for everyone? *Childhood Education, 74*(5), 283–292.

Mac Naughton, G. (1994). "You can be dad": Gender and power in domestic discourses and fantasy play within early childhood. *Journal for Australian Research in Early Childhood Education, 1,* 93–101.

Morris, D., Blanton, L., Blanton, W. E., Nowacek, J., & Perney J. (1995). Teaching low-achieving spellers at their instructional level. *The Elementary School Journal, 96* (2), 163–177.

Ochsner, M. B. (1999a, June). *Seeking power: The politics and practices of feminisms in early childhood education.* Paper presented at the eighth Interdisciplinary Conference Reconceptualizing Early Childhood Education: Research, Theory, and Practice, Ohio State University, Columbus.

Ochsner, M. B. (1999b). *Something rad and risque: A feminist poststructuralist study of gender in an urban kindergarten classroom.* Unpublished doctoral dissertation, Teachers College, Columbia University, New York.

Popkewitz, T. S. (1984). *Paradigm and ideology in educational research: The social functions of the individual.* London: Falmer.

Richardson, V. (1994). Conducting research on practice. *Educational Researcher, 23*(5), 5–10.

Ryan, S. K. (1998). *Freedom to choose: A post-structural study of child-centered pedagogy in a kindergarten classroom.* Unpublished doctoral dissertation, Teachers College, Columbia University, New York.

Schweinhart, L. J., & Weikhart, D. P. (1997). The High/Scope preschool curriculum comparison study through age 23. *Early Childhood Research Quarterly, 12,* 117–143.

Shulman, L. (1986). Paradigms and research programs in the study of teaching: A contemporary perspective. In M. C. Wittrock (Ed.), *Handbook of research on teaching* (3rd ed.; pp. 3–36). New York: Macmillan.

Stires, S. (1991). *With promise: Redefining reading and writing for "special" students.* Portsmouth, NH: Heinemann.

Tobin, J. (1995). Post-structural research in early childhood education. In J. A. Hatch (Ed.), *Qualitative research in early childhood settings* (pp. 223–243). Westport, CT: Praeger.

Wexler, P. (1987). *Social analysis of education: After the new sociology.* London: Methuen.

CHAPTER 4

Advocacy and Early Childhood Educators: Identity and Cultural Conflicts

Susan Grieshaber

FOR SOME TIME, early childhood education literature has supported the idea that early childhood educators should advocate and become activists for young children, their families, and the profession (e.g., Beck, 1979; Dimidjian, 1989; Fennimore, 1989; Goffin & Lombardi, 1988). A review of the advocacy literature identifies ways in which early childhood professionals might work on behalf of young children, both inside and outside the classroom. This chapter explores how child advocacy contrasts with the ways in which early childhood educators are positioned in their daily work with young children as defined by the dominant discourse of developmentally appropriate practice (DAP) (Bredekamp, 1987; Bredekamp & Copple, 1997). Those who work with young children are positioned by this dominant discourse as nurturing, caring, supportive, and responsive to the needs and interests of individual children. In contrast, the child advocacy literature exhorts staff to take risks, engage in confrontational behavior, be willing to engage in conflict, as well as to critique and negotiate.

This chapter argues that both the advocacy literature and the professional literature are based on psychological constructs that understand individuals in particular ways. Contradictions between the two discourses are explained from a feminist poststructuralist perspective that incorporates human ambiguity and introduces the notion of multiple identities. The chapter concludes that early childhood educators can satisfy the challenges of both bodies of literature through an understanding of multiple identities. However, this requires a theoretical perspective from outside developmental psychology. Data from two case examples show how pain and uncertainty are an integral part of any decision to adopt alternative perspectives and challenge what is taken for granted.

ADVOCACY

Advocacy literature has been part of early childhood education for some time. In 1984 Caldwell argued that advocacy was the responsibility of every member of the early childhood field, while Simons (1986) described advocacy as leadership about issues related to the broader context of early childhood education. As might be expected, advocacy has been defined in a variety of ways, with some explanations focusing on the process itself and some identifying what advocacy might mean for the profession. For instance, Goffin and Lombardi (1988) state that early childhood advocacy "means standing up for children and their needs" (p. 1). Fennimore (1989) has provided a more complex understanding of advocacy as

> a personal commitment to active involvement in the lives of children beyond remunerated professional responsibilities with the goal of enhancing the opportunities of those children for optimal personal growth and development. For early childhood professionals, child advocacy is the way in which they take their dedication to the service of young children as a step (or many steps) further to the point of becoming activists for young children. (p. 4)

Writing from the perspective of parents, Beck (1979) saw early childhood advocacy as "an attitude, a process you go through, and all the steps along the way that bring about changes to help children grow and develop fully" (p. 12). More recently, Lindamood (1995) has offered a continuum of advocacy for those who work with young children, identifying a range of five levels of involvement from dreamer through fighter. Each level entails "increasing amounts of personal involvement and risk" (p. 23). Advocacy also has been linked with ideas of leadership and the professionalism of early childhood educators (Fennimore, 1989; Lindamood, 1995; Rodd, 1994, 1997; Simons, 1986), while Gnezda (1996) has said that early childhood educators must advocate on behalf of children at the level of state and local policy making in relation to welfare reform.

Many who have written about early childhood advocacy exhort those working with young children to take action on behalf of young children, their families, and the profession. In relating some of the ways in which those working with young children have been urged to act, my purpose is to identify some features of what has been written about advocacy and not to critique the content itself. For example, in the preface to their book, Goffin and Lombardi (1988) state explicitly, "This book is a call to action" (p. v). A little later they say, "Children need us to vote, to lobby, to inform, and to speak out on their behalf" (p. 1). Dimidjian (1989), too, ensures that early childhood educators understand that the fate of children rests with action (or lack thereof): "The activist/advocate early childhood educator works to bring concern for and commitment to vulnerable young lives to the forefront in the wider social community" (p. 54). Perhaps most emphatic is the writing of Fennimore (1989), who stated:

> A good early childhood educator must be a strong and compassionate person. . . . Educators must believe that they can, by the sheer power of their own planning and will, make a lasting change for the better in children. . . . Educators must be trained to recognize, believe in, and practice their own power to stand up for children in society. They must learn that they are responsible, in all they do, for the protection and well-being of children in society. They must learn that teachers do not quit or absolve themselves of responsibility when their students experience difficulties and setbacks. (p. xii–xiii)

Although not as strongly expressed as the ideas of Fennimore, other literature about early childhood advocacy generally entreats workers to speak and take action on behalf of children.

While advocacy is a worthwhile pursuit for early childhood professionals, there appears to be some contradiction between what early childhood educators are urged to do as advocates, and the way in which developmentally appropriate practice positions early childhood professionals in their daily work with young children.

THE DISCOURSE OF DEVELOPMENTALLY APPROPRIATE PRACTICE

Located within the paradigm of developmental psychology, developmentally appropriate practice (DAP) swiftly became the dominant discourse following the original publication by Bredekamp (1987) on behalf of the U.S. National Association for the Education of Young Children (NAEYC). This NAEYC position statement was followed by a plethora of written materials supporting developmentally appropriate practice, numerous critiques of the concept (e.g., Mallory & New, 1994), and a revised edition of the statement (Bredekamp & Copple, 1997). A testament to the dominance of the discourse of developmentally appropriate practice is the sale of more than half a million copies of the 1987 position statement, the distribution of several million brochures about DAP, and the adoption of DAP by numerous state departments of education in the United States and several other countries, including Australia, New Zealand, and the province of British Columbia in Canada (Bredekamp & Copple, 1997, p. v).

My comments here are restricted to the way in which early childhood staff are positioned by the dominant discourse of developmentally appropriate practice in their daily work with young children. By this I mean the way in which the discourse of DAP both explicitly and implicitly prescribes the parameters of what those adults who work with young children are supposed to do and how they are supposed to do it. I now provide some examples.

In defining developmentally appropriate practice, Bredekamp and Copple (1997) state that it is the outcome of

> a process of teacher decision making that draws on at least three critical, interrelated bodies of knowledge: (1) what teachers know about how children develop and learn; (2) what teachers know about the individual children in their group; and (3) knowledge of the social and cultural context in which those children live and learn. (p. vii)

The purpose of teaching is "to enhance development and learning" (p. 17), and ways in which this is to occur are specified throughout Bredekamp and Copple's book. For example, teachers are to be responsive to "children's differing needs, interests, styles and abilities" (p. 17) and to provide children with "meaningful choice and time to explore through active involvement" (p. 18). Patience is considered an important attribute for teachers (p. 19), particularly in relation to reminding children about rules and their rationale. In addition, teachers "must support a positive sense of self-identity in each child" (p. 40).

Adults working with infants are required to be sensitive and demonstrate interest in understanding infants (p. 63); a special relationship should exist between the caregiver and the infant: "Like dancers, the caregiver and the infant synchronize their interactions, each responding to and influencing the other" (p. 58). In relation to toddlers, the skilled caregiver offers experiences that support initiative, creativity, autonomy, and self-esteem. Yet she [the caregiver] recognizes that while striving to be independent and self-reliant, toddlers count on the understanding and vigilance of the adults who love them. (p. 68)

Bredekamp and Copple identify many examples of appropriate practices for teachers of children aged 3 to 5, again focusing on the portrayal of adults as warm, gentle, supportive, responsive, patient, encouraging, and facilitating beings who patiently redirect and guide children in their development and learning. For example, "teachers are patient, realizing that not every minor infraction warrants a response" (p. 129), and teachers recognize that "learning experiences are more effective when the curriculum is responsive to the children's interests and ideas as they emerge" (p. 131).

There is some contrast, however, between the characteristics required of adults within the discourse of developmental appropriateness and attributes that have been described as necessary in advocating for young children. On the one hand, adults working with young children within the dominant discourse are constituted as nurturing and responsive to their charges. Advocacy, on the other hand, "often involves conflict, confrontation, and negotiation" (Goffin & Lombardi, 1988, p. 9). It appears as though there is a contradiction between the skills that advocates require, and the preferred version of adult interaction with young children as evidenced by the discourse of developmentally appropriate practice.

An example of what Mead (in Rodd, 1997) has called "better practice" provides another perspective that can be located between the position of early childhood staff as advocates and that of developmentally appropriate practice. Mead has argued that better practice involves "a 'warm demander', that is a professional, competent teacher" (p. 3), who is warm and responsive but also capable of demanding learning and competence. The use of the term *warm demander* encapsulates the dichotomy described previously between the way in which the discourse of developmentally appropriate practice constitutes adults who work with young children on a daily basis, and the characteristics required by early childhood advocates.

THE INDIVIDUAL SUBJECT

A focus on the individual child is one of the central tenets of developmental psychology. Early childhood educators understand young children as individual learners, interacting with them as separate beings and basing their teaching decisions on each child's needs, interests, and abilities. These understandings about individuals are based on humanism and evidenced in much child-centered curriculum as well as the aspect of progressivism that focuses on individualism (Pinar, Reynolds, Slattery, & Taubman, 1995). In theories such as humanism, the individual subject is described as pre-given, unified, rational, and encompassing a fixed and unchanging perspective. What this means is that the subject is seen as an "unchanging human essence that precedes all social operations" (Best & Kellner, 1991, p. 51). Weedon (1997) described the humanist subject as "something at the heart of the individual which is unique, fixed and coherent and which makes her what she *is*" (p. 32, emphasis in original), the essential individual.

In feminist poststructuralism there can be no essentialist understandings of notions such as woman, man, early childhood educator, and childhood. Such understandings always change over time and in different situations and are "historically produced through a range of discursive practices" (Weedon, 1997, p. 146). This means, for example, that there are no permanent and essential attributes of early childhood educators that are consistent across all histories and contexts. Likewise, there are no pre-existing characteristics of early childhood staff that represent truth regardless of circumstances. Understandings about early childhood educators are defined differently in every culture, in every time period, and in each political, economic, and social context. What we know and understand about early childhood educators is context specific.

The humanist notion of the unified rational subject is problematic when the discourse of advocacy and the discourse of developmentally appropriate practice are considered, as teachers are placed in contradictory positions by each discourse. Teachers are supposed to meet children's needs through nurturance and care, and at the same time are urged to advocate for children, knowing that such advocacy may involve contestation and conflict. From a humanist perspective, this is a theoretical challenge. While it is possible to be a warm demander as Mead has suggested, accounting for this requires a theoretical shift from the way the subject is understood in humanism. I now investigate this apparent contradiction further, seeking resolution by turning to the position of feminist poststructuralism and the way in which subjectivity is understood within this theoretical approach.

FEMINIST POSTSTRUCTURALISM

A feminist poststructuralist approach (introduced in Chapter 1) uses principles of poststructuralism and aspects of feminism in an attempt to account for relationships between the individual and the social (Weedon, 1997). Poststructuralism provides an awareness of how power relations within society operate in particular ways (Foucault, 1977). When combined with gender, a feminist poststructuralist approach seeks understanding of how power relations in society are gendered. Of particular relevance to my discussion is the notion of multiple identities or contradictory subjectivity, made possible by both feminist and poststructural theoretical approaches. Through theorizing the notion of multiple identities, it is possible for early childhood professionals to be warm demanders and satisfy the requirements of the literature relating to both advocacy and developmentally appropriate practice.

Contradictory Subjectivity

According to Mac Naughton (1998), subjectivity "describes who we are and how we understand ourselves. These understandings are formed as we participate in, articulate and circulate discourse" (p. 161). Understanding subjectivity as socially constructed means that it is not something essential or innate (as in humanist perspectives) or something that is genetically determined (as in biological perspectives). Instead the subjectivity of individuals is constructed and produced in the political, social, and economic circumstances (discourses) currently operating in society. It also involves the mind, body, and emotions. The discourse of developmentally appropriate practice and the discourse of advocacy position early childhood educators in different ways by producing different subject positions for the individuals involved. As Mac Naughton (1998) has said, "Discourses form subjectivity, they constitute the very foundations upon which early childhood staff choices are made about what to do, what not to do, how to do it and who to do it with" (p. 161).

In a feminist poststructuralist approach, language plays a central role: Language "is not the expression of unique individuality; it constructs the individual's subjectivity in ways which are socially specific" (Weedon, 1997, p. 21). In humanist approaches, subjectivity is understood as fixed. In poststructuralist approaches, subjectivity is theorized as "precarious, contradictory and in process, constantly being reconstituted in discourse each time we think or speak" (Weedon, 1997, p. 32). Subjectivity, then, can be understood as a range of subjectivities (or identities) that are mediated by certain discourses in particular ways. For example, the discourse of developmentally appropriate practice constructs and produces early childhood staff to be warm and nurturing. The formation of subjectivity is experienced and established by adopting a variety of discursive identities, some of which may conflict with each other (antagonisms or contradictory subjectivity) and some of which exist in relative harmony.

Individuals are therefore sites where struggles occur, with these struggles taking "place in the consciousness of the individual" (Weedon, 1997, p. 106). Early childhood educators, for example, may struggle between being positioned as warm and nurturing in the discourse of developmentally appropriate practice and being positioned as potentially confrontational in the advocacy discourse. Persons establish and experience their own individuality by adopting a variety of discursive subjectivities (identities), which are not necessarily harmonious.

We all have had experiences of contradictory subjectivity, where different identities do not exist harmoniously. To illustrate the point, I now use two specific examples about one teacher and one teacher educator. As a means of explaining contradictory subjectivity, I share some of the difficulties faced by those attempting to move beyond constructions of early childhood educators as warm nurturers in their daily work with and for young children. The pain and uncertainty of moving from the accepted or dominant position to adopt a different approach are clearly demonstrated in each case.

An Early Childhood Teacher

The first example is drawn from Miller's (1992) writing about Georgette, one of the teachers with whom Miller had been collaborating for 6 years on a research project. Georgette was attempting to reconcile the difference between being constructed as a woman and as a teacher, and therefore as warm and nurturing, with "becoming vocal" and exploring "the nature and possible forms of [her] own 'authority' in ways that do not reinforce or replicate unequal power relationships" (p. 106). Miller commented on Georgette's struggle:

> Georgette's particular struggle to reposition herself within her elementary school as both a caring, nurturing teacher and a questioning, challenging educator reflects many educators' difficulties not only with hierarchies of schooling but also with the gender-specified roles that we are expected to play within those hierarchies. (pp. 108–109)

Miller (1992) used Pagano's work with those in the research project to help them understand that "for women who teach, there need be no conflict between nurturance and authority if women can acknowledge, critique, and work to move through the power of masculinist totalizing discourses" (p. 107). The discourse of nurturance and caring for women teachers remains very powerful, in much the same way as does the discourse of developmentally appropriate practice. An alternative position in which women teachers are authoritative is difficult to achieve because of the taken-for-granted understandings of caring that accompany being a female teacher.

Choosing to be both nurturing and authoritative turned out to be a struggle for Georgette. As indicated by Pagano (in Miller, 1992), working through contradictory positions can achieve convergence between nurturance and authority. However, for Georgette, the process was a difficult and painful experience:

> I know that I have changed as a result of our work together, changed from an accepting, docile teacher, to a questioning, challenging person. . . . With this comes the realization that some people with whom I work are uneasy and uncomfortable around me. Perhaps I've become the unexpected and others are unsure how to "handle" me. For me, "handle" means suppress, control, or keep me in my place. I know that it is my thinking that offends them. I am in turmoil, struggling to exist and not be made quiet again. (Miller, 1992, p. 108)

It appears as though Georgette made a conscious decision to change from being a docile and accepting teacher to one who questioned and challenged the status quo. Her decision involved a change in subjectivity from being positioned through discourse as a caring elementary teacher, the accepted or taken-for-granted position for a female teacher, to a position that was more authoritative and questioning. However, the cost of her decision was high both personally and professionally.

Although struggling to exist, Georgette did not want to be silenced again and resisted being repositioned discursively by others as a means of "handling" her. This is an example of how Georgette and others have been regulated by the discourse that produces women teachers as caring and nurturing. Attempts by Georgette to challenge and resist that discourse gave rise to efforts from others at her school to keep her in her place. Here it is possible to see the discursive social practices and gendered understandings operating at Georgette's school. Georgette has a large emotional investment in her changed position, but surviving the discursive pressure put on her caused her enormous turmoil.

An Early Childhood Teacher Educator

The second example is drawn from Ryan (1997), where she described teaching a class in a New York university as a part-time professor. The class had been discussing some of the biases inherent in Piaget's theory, when one of the students asked: "Why have I had to study and recite the theories of Piaget all year when you're now telling me his ideas are not relevant nor in the best interests of kids?" The class became silent, and Ryan found herself "fumbling through thoughts to find what might be a correct response" (p. 3). She described how she physically checked by looking outside the classroom door to see if any other members of the faculty were in the vicinity of the classroom lest they hear her response. Ryan then said, "To be honest I'm not sure why most of us persist in conveying these ideas to our students" (p. 3).

Like Georgette, Ryan (1997) struggled with many issues, at the base of which was contradictory subjectivity. As teacher (professor), Ryan was positioned to present taken-for-granted knowledge as part of the course. By challenging the accepted position, Ryan moved outside the discourse, adopting a contradictory position. Ryan appeared aware of the risks, indicated by her action of checking outside the classroom before speaking further. She positioned herself as questioning the continued teaching of particular Piagetian ideas when such ideas were considered contrary to the best interests of children.

Making the statement that the "teacher education program was not necessarily presenting her [the student] with the most up-to-date knowledge" (p. 13) left Ryan in the position of failing to defend those who were responsible for the course. It also positioned her as challenging the status quo, questioning the unquestioned, that is, questioning the acceptance of privileging certain knowledge. Ryan also felt she was unable to act on her "own convictions that much of the content of our teacher education course required revision" (p. 13). While such self-reflective accounts indicate where discursive boundaries within the academy are located, they also indicate what is at stake in adopting a contradictory position.

Although Ryan indicated an understanding of the power relations operating in the academy and some of the effects of the contradictory ways in which she was positioned, this should not detract from the emotional investment and the potentially high cost of her actions. The prevailing social practices worked against the presentation of alternative perspectives, positioning Ryan as resisting the accepted procedures and processes of the academy, but also as not daring to speak before physically checking outside the door.

CONCLUSION

From a theoretical perspective, the conceptualization of contradictory subjectivity or multiple identities is relatively uncomplicated. The significant point is that theorizing about being a warm demander, or a nurturer with authority, is the straightforward part. The hard part is enacting the theory: What personal and professional cost is there to individuals attempting to adopt positions that are different from those that are accepted and taken for granted? Is it worth it, and will the participants have the strength to endure the personal and professional costs of being positioned by colleagues as resistant, hard to handle, and questioning? Some understanding of the confusion and conflict endured by both Georgette (Miller, 1992) and Ryan (1997) was evident in the short excerpts from their stories.

A feminist poststructuralist theoretical perspective enables reconciliation between the two seemingly disparate positions of caregiver as advocate and as warm nurturer. The excerpts provided insight into the complexities and emotional turmoil that often come with challenging taken-for-granted ways of doing things. There are ways in which early childhood educators can be both warm demanders and authoritative nurturers without feeling that they have compromised advocacy or developmentally appropriate practice. Likewise, there are ways that early childhood educators can challenge accepted ways of doing things by adopting alternative approaches. However, adopting alternative approaches comes at a huge emotional, personal, and professional cost. As teacher educators, we can provide opportunities for students to engage in ideas about contradictory subjectivity, by providing examples from the field and offering them for analysis and discussion. In relation to this chapter, some examples include the following:

1. Discuss the notion of a warm demander. Consider whether students think it is possible and how they may achieve what they consider a good balance for them between nurturing and being authoritative. What personal costs might be involved?
2. Encourage students to talk to early childhood teachers they may know who have been struggling with making changes or adopting different perspectives from those considered usual in early childhood education. Think about institutional constraints, emotional investment, and personal and professional risks involved. Discuss how these teachers may have worked through such changes given the constraints and risks involved.

3. Discuss the importance of early childhood educators being open to interpreting from different vantage points.

The primary advantage in examining and perhaps adopting alternative ways of knowing and doing would appear to be that interpreting from other vantage points offers ways of personal, professional, and cultural renewal (Greene, 1988).

REFERENCES

Beck, R. (1979). *It's time to stand up for your children: A parent's guide to child advocacy.* Washington, DC: Children's Defense Fund.

Best, S., & Kellner, D. (1991). *Postmodern theory: Critical interrogations.* London: Macmillan.

Bredekamp, S. (1987). *Developmentally appropriate practice in early childhood programs serving children from birth through age 8.* Washington, DC: National Association for the Education of Young Children.

Bredekamp, S., & Copple, C. (1997). *Developmentally appropriate practice in early childhood programs serving children from birth through age 8* (rev. ed.). Washington, DC: National Association for the Education of Young Children.

Caldwell, B. (1984). Advocacy is everybody's business. *Child Care Information Exchange, 54,* 29–32.

Dimidjian, J. (1989). *Early childhood at risk: Actions and advocacy for young children.* Washington, DC: National Education Association.

Fennimore, B. S. (1989). *Child advocacy for early childhood educators.* New York: Teachers College Press.

Foucault, M. (1977). *Discipline and punish: The birth of the prison* (A. Sheridan, Trans.). Harmondsworth, England: Penguin.

Gnezda, M. T. (1996). Welfare reform: Personal responsibilities and opportunities for early childhood advocates. *Young Children, 52*(1), 55–58.

Goffin, S., & Lombardi, J. (1988). *Speaking out: Early childhood advocacy.* Washington, DC: National Association for the Education of Young Children.

Greene, M. (1988). *The dialectic of freedom.* New York: Teachers College Press.

Lindamood, J. B. (1995). Teachers as child advocates: A continuum of involvement. *Day Care and Early Education, 22*(4), 23–24.

Mac Naughton, G., (1998). Improving our gender equity tools: A case for discourse analysis. In N. Yelland (Ed.), *Gender in early childhood* (pp. 149–174). London: Routledge.

Mallory, B. L., & New, R. S. (1994). *Diversity and developmentally appropriate practices: Challenges for early childhood education*. New York: Teachers College Press.

Miller, J. (1992). Teachers, autobiography, and curriculum: Critical and feminist perspectives. In S. Kessler & B. B. Swadener (Eds.), *Reconceptualizing the early childhood curriculum: Beginning the dialogue* (pp. 102–122). New York: Teachers College Press.

Pinar, W. F., Reynolds, W. M., Slattery, P., & Taubman, P. M. (1995). *Understanding curriculum: An introduction to the study of historical and contemporary curriculum discourses*. New York: Peter Lang.

Rodd, J. (1994). *Leadership in early childhood: The pathway to professionalism*. St. Leonards, NSW: Allen & Unwin; New York: Teachers College Press.

Rodd, J. (1997). Learning to develop as early childhood professionals. *Australian Journal of Early Childhood, 22*(1), 1–5.

Ryan, S. (1997, September). *Rethinking the developmental foundations of early childhood teacher education*. Paper presented at the Australian Early Childhood Association National Conference, Melbourne.

Simons, J. (1986). *Administering early childhood services*. Sydney: Southwood Press.

Weedon, C. (1997). *Feminist practice and poststructuralist theory* (2nd ed.). Oxford: Basil Blackwell.

CHAPTER 5

A Reconstructed Tale of Inclusion for a Lesbian Family in an Early Childhood Classroom

Janice Kroeger

IN THIS CHAPTER, I use a series of events from my teaching to convey the dissonance created by several compelling conflicts. I point out pedagogic recommendations cited in research against the backdrop of social complexity represented by one rural classroom community. I explicate roles that I took as a professional educator, in contrast to those of the parents, who were local experts with a unique understanding of their own community. Pedagogic conflict and interactive or shifting identities and behaviors of teachers, children, and parents are used here to reinterpret several happenings. The end product is a deceptively simple framework for conveying a series of epistemological problems, which seemed at that time to have no clear-cut or perfect solutions.

I tell a story about a child in my class named Caleb. He is what could be called a "historical child" (Graue & Walsh, 1998). Caleb is positioned in a controversial and evolving educational movement, approximated by the changing literature in the field. In this piece, I reveal my own sexual identity as a bisexual teacher, because I believe it helped me to understand the tensions that Caleb's lesbian parents experienced when representing themselves in our school. By revealing my teaching position in this chapter, I am able to signify the challenges that teachers face when implementing socially just curricula.

Through writing this chapter, I have gained a new understanding of Caleb and his parents, Joan and Bobbie. Both women have conferred with me through telephone conversations about the events. They have assisted me as I have attempted to develop this narrative for retelling.

SEARCHING THE LITERATURE: GAY/LESBIAN FAMILY INCLUSION

The literature of anti-bias curriculum (Derman-Sparks, 1989) specifically challenged educators to expand children's ideas of identity and to counteract racism, sexism, handicappism, classism, and homophobia as they occurred in the early childhood classroom. When educators adjust their teaching to resist bias, children are believed in turn to resist bias in themselves and in their peers (Derman-Sparks, 1989; Rainbow Curriculum as described in Miller-Lachmann & Taylor, 1995; *Starting Small: Teaching Tolerance in Preschool and the Early Grades* from the Southern Poverty Law Center [SPLC], 1997). These three widely available resources reflect an early childhood vision of teaching for social justice, in which teachers and students are asked to change their "world views" of events and each other (Adams, Bell, & Griffin, 1997), and to change oppressive structures in the classroom.

It is important to note that at least two pedagogic tools underlie anti-bias curriculum, Rainbow Curriculum, and *Starting Small: Teaching Tolerance in Preschool and the Early Grades*. First, each curriculum approach relies on complex discussions and interactions between individuals in the classroom as a leading activity for individual and group change and social action. Pivotal discussions initiated by teachers are to reflect the increasingly diverse populations of schools and the unique contributions that an array of individuals brings to communities. Discussions meet the increasingly complex needs of young children as they develop the ability to think critically, act, and respond responsibly toward others that may be or may not be similar to themselves (SPLC, 1997). Second, these socially just perspectives emphasize giving children images of diversity. Seeing other children in uncommon family arrangements, for example, can provide the group with a reflection of various lived realities. A fairly recent text, *Valuing Diversity: The Primary Years* (Brown McCracken, 1993), explains that children who are least likely to see images like themselves are children of color; those who are poor, homeless, or have disabilities; and those whose families contradict dominant views. Recommendations stress that children need to see images of their own experience (Brown McCracken, 1993).

Discussions of sexuality emerged in particular early childhood curricular materials during the late 1980s and early 1990s and interlaced with discussions of social justice. Further, some multicultural education texts revealed subtle shifts both in *inclusions* and in *representations* of sexual identity. Themes in some multicultural texts nested gay/lesbian/bisexual and transgendered (GLBT) concerns under items such as sexual preference or factors comprising cultural diversity, sexual orientation, and teaching for diversity (Cordeiro, Reagan, & Martinez, 1994). Available multicultural resources threaded the issues of GLBT individuals and schools throughout texts devoted to oppressed groups (Sleeter & Grant, 1994).

Home and school relationship texts, on the other hand, did not address gay and lesbian families until the very late 1990s. Racial, class, marital, and linguistic status historically have been explicit (Balster-Liontos, 1992; Epstein, Coates, Salinas, Sanders, & Simon, 1996; Graue, 1993; Lareau & Horvatt, 1999; Reglin, 1993; Swap, 1993), but there has been little reference to the presence of gay- or lesbian-headed families. More recently, home and school research has identified the lesbian and gay family under a larger rubric of diversity (Fuller & Olson, 1998). The gay/lesbian family is described as "conspicuous and more numerous, . . . controversial" (p. 25), and plagued with "a societal hesitation to label them as family" (p. 45). This recent research suggests that staff and teachers are to "remain nonjudgmental and open to family involvement, even when a family is nontraditional" (Warner, 1998, p. 30).

In addition to these resources, a form of sexuality education was addressed more fully in a body of very specific literature that included a range of student ages and educational contexts during the latter half of the 1990s. Scholarship was initiated at that time that promoted teaching approaches that gave "voice" to the complex social realities of children and teachers (Clay, 1990; Silin, 1995). Much of this research suggested that teachers would have to address concerns about sexual orientation and students coming out at younger ages, as well as issues of visibility dealt with by gay/lesbian families (Casper, Cuffaro, Schultz, Silin, & Wickens, 1996). More generally, researchers predicted that the training of teachers in elementary schools and high schools would become increasingly complex surrounding sexuality education and the teacher's role (Hulsebosch & Koerner, 1997; Sears, 1994). Finally, very recently, the intersection of gay/lesbian family life and school experience has been theorized (Casper & Schultz, 1999).

I searched the literature for the dilemmas I faced in teaching 4-year-old Caleb and working with his parents. The historical present perspective in the literature from the early 1990s is concurrent with the time that is described in the story; yet, our situation did not fit neatly with any of the emergent recommendations in the research literature.

OUR STORY OF INCLUSION

Anti-bias curriculum and multicultural ideology provided me with a unifying element for the diverse community of young children (ages 3–6) who were my students. While other teachers developed units based around primarily traditional European American holidays and general concepts, my co-teacher Phyllis and I discussed and agreed to enact a multicultural or anti-bias curriculum. We attempted to show children a multiplicity of racial, intergenerational, ability, and social class images. Our messages to children about families were that they were all different, but that in our classroom we would accept and talk about family variations and try to understand them. We relied heavily on selectively chosen books, toys, posters, and manipulatives that directly fostered inclusive understandings. In the context of arranging images of more typical types of families, I found an absence of commercially produced images depicting lesbian or gay families. So, I would mix and match paper cutouts of two adult males with a child or two adult women with a child or two. Over the 8 years I taught, children never said no to my query of whether or not this arrangement could be a family. Our practices did not represent a transformational curriculum, but could be described as an additive or a contributions approach (Banks & Banks, 1993, in Miller-Lachmann & Taylor, 1995). However, these practices provided a foundation upon which I have come to understand the concepts of "activism" and classroom transformation differently.

Meeting Caleb

> JOAN: You mean you knew of us before you came to the classroom? Hey, wait a minute. How come you knew us, and we didn't know you? What did you know about us before you came to be a teacher here? (Telephone conversation with Bobbie and Joan, Summer 1997)

As I was to begin my sixth year of teaching, I was told that Caleb, a 4-year-old child whose older brother Jonathan was in the same school, would be my student. Caleb's mother, Joan, had brought both boys into the world by artificial insemination. Joan was a self-employed mom and spent lots of time in the school volunteering. On all paperwork and in person, Joan represented herself as a single parent. But, Bobbie, a middle-aged woman, was also a part of the children's lives. I learned through my supervisor that Bobbie shared a home with Joan and the children, and was herself a second-grade teacher.

My initial interpretation for Joan's choice of representation on paperwork was that she made a decision to conceal a lesbian family identity. I looked forward to working with Caleb and began planning specific elements of the curriculum that would reflect the uniqueness of Caleb's family life. I bought the book *Heather Has Two Mommies* (Neuman, 1989) with the intent to use it in the classroom.

Caleb's World

> JOAN: I knew you didn't get it when I tried to explain how it was here. If you are going to tell a story at least get it right! They [the community] will get you one way or another.

In the classroom, during a collage/literacy project depicting how children came to school, Caleb told me in a soft voice that mommy drove him. I wrote this for him on his project. Then Caleb, upon seeing the selection of vehicle cutouts available, commented that Bobbie also "had a truck." Caleb made a second collage and informed me that "Bobbie had a gun." I nodded. Then he judiciously added that "Bobbie also takes care of the horses, and that hers will buck." In his first days of school, Caleb communicated to me and confirmed the supervisor's assessment that Bobbie was a powerful player in his life. Later in the week, Joan brought the collage back to me with *the correct spelling of Bobbie's name* (rather than the male-oriented "Bobby"). I stapled this to the hallway display strip with all of the others.

I noticed throughout the first weeks of school that Joan remained distant, eyes sometimes averted, and Caleb remained quiet as well. I began to suspect on the basis of Joan's coolness to me, during arrival and pickup times, that she was indifferent to me either as Caleb's teacher or as a potential family supportive ally. After many weeks of my greetings, smiles, and detailed reports of Caleb's progress, I suggested that I would like to know them better through a home visit.

The book *Heather Has Two Mommies* remained in my bag. I wondered whether it was appropriate for *them* to read this book as a family, rather than for me to read it in the more public arena of the classroom. I wondered *how* Joan talked about Bobbie and her relationship to the boys. I imagined that if Caleb did not see his mother being friendly with me, his first teacher, then this could damage his eventual trust of other teachers in the school. More centrally, how would Caleb's understanding of his family come to be compared *in his eyes* with the worth of other children's families? I concluded that what was a socially confusing dynamic to me, might be even more so to Caleb. I wondered to myself what this closeted family existence would eventually bring to Caleb, his brother, and Bobbie and Joan's cohesiveness as a family unit. Joan agreed that I should come for a home visit.

As I drove from a visit to a home that was middle-income and fundamentalist Christian, to a home that experienced chronic poverty, and then to Caleb's house, I marveled at the contrasts between each child and the family situations in our classrooms. Caleb's house was large and had many cabinets of toys, a swimming pool, and a barn with horses. I learned that the boys had many material things that other children in our classroom did not. In addition, Caleb and his brother did not always get along well in their mother's eyes, but usually got along well enough. I also learned that Bobbie's physical and emotional presence was essential to making their family work. In particular, I learned that Bobbie helped Jonathan learn to read, she took the boys to Sunday school, and, in Caleb's words, "went shopping for Mommy, when Mommy was rusted out." There was a family picture on the wall, and "Bobbie and Joan" knickknacks over the fireplace. In addition, I learned that the neighbors did not allow their children to walk the short distance down the road to play with the boys, who then "kept to themselves." I also learned that their house had been vandalized, and in the distant past people that Joan and Bobbie did not know in the small neighboring town had been verbally abusive.

Acting in Relationship

> JOAN: I knew [you were] different when you asked that question about prejudice.

After this visit to Caleb's house, I reinterpreted what it might mean for Joan and Bobbie to do anything but remain a quiet presence in this community. My understanding of their family was that they provided a secure environment and a broad range of opportunities for their children, which included swimming, gymnastics, scout activities, and T-ball. The division of household and economic responsibilities as well as the emotional climate between Bobbie and Joan seemed to reflect what educators would hope for in children's families. Yet, paradoxically, the very functional behaviors that I interpreted as necessary for Caleb's development were the very things that Joan and Bobbie appeared to me to conceal from the world of the school. I learned that rendering themselves less visible as a family to the school was a functional choice. Bobbie called this "laying low." In their case, laying low meant they avoided questions from people by distancing. Although distancing didn't allow them close relationships in the school community, it did allow them to eliminate potential contact with individuals who might prove untrustworthy.

I had to rethink how I might be making Caleb's family more vulnerable by my presence in the school. My inclination to use the presence of Caleb's family as a leading activity of educating others about this lesbian family seemed ludicrous against the backdrop of open hostility that Joan described. Coming to know Bobbie and Joan made me question my understandings of what was best for Caleb (and myself) in circumstances of potential homophobic backlash from the surrounding community. I weighed heavily the many possible social consequences of representing Caleb's family to the other children. In this case, presenting images of Bobbie and Joan as a couple might have violated their own parental code of conduct, which was purposeful and protective both to Caleb and his brother and to themselves.

The moments with Caleb's family challenged my understanding of anti-bias teaching. I questioned myself as a lesbian-identified teacher. My basic beliefs about my role here as an early childhood educator were disrupted, and above all my former thoughts of approaching and presenting Caleb's family to others in this school and community were shattered. I questioned the efficacy of my past actions in which I had represented images of a same-gender couple symbolically to young children, against this paradoxical but real situation, in which the lesbian family that I intended to support seemed to wish to remain invisible. Bobbie's and Joan's presence made me vulnerable in ways that I had not known before as a bisexual teacher. I became less comfortable day by day in developing or implementing a dynamic and socially reflective curriculum for our children.

Negotiating Discomfort

JOAN: People are always asking, "Who are you?" From the Sunday school staff when she takes them . . .

BOBBIE: I always take them. And I tell people: "I am Bobbie."

JOAN: And they say, "Yes, but who are you?"

BOBBIE: From their teachers! "Who are you?" Do you believe

that? Do you know I have to have a note from Joan to pick
them up? Isn't that stupid? I can't believe it; I have to have a
note! I have been with these kids since they were born. I
changed their diapers, and I have to have a note. I'm Bobbie!
"Are you their grandmother?" No, I am Bobbie. "Are you
their aunt?" No, I'm Bobbie! Everybody has to have a category. It's a matter of having categories. They don't have one,
they can't find one, and they can't make one up. The boys
don't need a category. Sometimes one of them just comes
up, puts his arms around me, and tells me, "I'm so glad I
have you for my Bobbie."

Ultimately in our classroom, I did not want Caleb to think that
there was anything wrong with him or them because of Bobbie's role.
In the classroom, I told Phyllis and our assistant Mary Beth that I
didn't know what experiences Caleb's brother had in the school or
what would happen in subsequent grades, but we would talk to Caleb
about his family matter-of-factly, and often, and without a sense of
implied negative judgment.

I tried to have accurate and appropriate conversations with Caleb
personally, but found even there I was amiss. For example, in a conversation with Caleb and his peers about fathers, I commented to Caleb
that he didn't have a daddy, but that he had Bobbie. Caleb corrected
my ignorance by stating, "I do have a daddy, everyone has a daddy."
I realized Bobbie and Joan were doing a better job of educating Caleb
than I could. I responded, "You are right, Caleb, everyone has a Dad;
yours doesn't live with you." Caleb nodded, satisfied that I'd finally
gotten it right.

> BOBBIE: Sometimes the boys talk about having a father, and
> when that happens we try to do all the things a father might
> do with them, build that tree-house, go fishing, Caleb loves
> fishing . . .
> JOAN: But when I remind them that if we had a daddy we
> wouldn't have Bobbie, that ends that conversation.

Throughout the early months of that year, despite my internal intellectual upheaval, I continued to listen to and talk with Caleb. I
noted that he seemed more comfortable and active. He had chosen a
few first friends and was beginning to take an interest in writing his
name for the first time.

The book *Heather Has Two Mommies* stayed in my locker. In those early months, my enthusiasm for teaching waned in the face of what I considered a significant compromise of one of my basic philosophies of practice (that students should see realistic *images* of themselves and others like them). I doubted my presence in teaching and began to "lay low" in our curriculum. During the class unit on "family," typically a favorite of mine and the children's, I chose a support role. Phyllis represented Caleb's family accurately and matter-of-factly. My interpretation is that Phyllis's status as a heterosexual middle-aged divorced woman allowed her to find the neutrality that exists in reporting children's social realities. I was pleased at this turn of events, but realized the depth of my own vulnerability. I silently watched Phyllis's lesson and contemplated that Bobbie and Joan's circumstance was now my own. I did not feel safe teaching, and I chose to remain silent in the face of a much larger internal and structurally forced sexual oppression.

Talking Bobbie In

Children were beginning to discuss our school's upcoming October Open House. At the sand table, several children were talking about who would be attending the celebration. Children volunteered information about expected family members; Caleb quietly and resolutely claimed that Jonathan and Mom would come to the event, but that Bobbie would not. When I asked him why, he responded that "she just doesn't like them, that's all." I assured him that if she changed her mind about "not liking" Open Houses, we wanted her there. That day, I reminded Joan that I knew she called herself a single mother, but that if Bobbie decided to participate in the Open House we would welcome her. I continued to "talk Bobbie in" with Caleb for many days, but experienced a place of discomfort, ambiguity, and doubt.

The words that I used with Caleb and my ambivalence became a wedge holding the classroom door open for Bobbie to come in, and a powerful reminder for myself that I could leave teaching if I chose to. I left the school building each day uncomfortable, knowing that what I was not doing seemed to reinscribe the very heteronormative concepts of family and sexuality that I wished to be different for Caleb and his generation of classmates. I felt as if I had caved under the powerful force of a silent but genuine sexuality oppression. I questioned whether Bobbie and Joan would ever feel comfortable sharing their relationship in the school. I felt my integrity for myself as an early childhood teacher diminish in light of my beliefs and former practices.

The School Open House

> BOBBIE: I think you gave him self-confidence. It was like he pur-
> sued me in ways that he had never done before. It was like
> suddenly I was in Caleb's program. With Jonathan, I was not
> in his program, but with Caleb, it was like his confidence
> grew, and he just would not let me be about that Open
> House.

On the night of the Open House, the school was filled to capacity. At the height of the chaos, Caleb proudly walked in pulling Bobbie by the arm. She introduced herself to me briefly and then he dragged her away. Later in the evening, we invited everyone to play games in the gym. At one point, children and their families ran together one at a time under the parachute. We collectively raised the parachute as family groups took turns. To my delight, Joan, Caleb, Jonathan, and Bobbie participated with proud smiles.

The Open House became a place in which Caleb and his lesbian parent family could successfully coexist with other diverse families. I became willing at that moment to once again believe in teaching as socially transformational.

> BOBBIE: It's harder now to lay low. Since that year, Caleb's pre-
> school year, they let me know that they want me at the Open
> House. They want to show me this, and they want to show
> me that. Now the boys want me there. I've been to every one
> since then. It was like I was pulled in. I wasn't there, and
> then I was.
> JOAN: But was it them that didn't let you come to the Open
> House all those years, or was it you?

An Inconclusive End

Several short weeks after the Open House, a new early childhood classroom was opened in a distant community, to which I was moved. Upon my departure, Caleb and Joan gave me a gift of handmade purple candles, with a card signed by Bobbie as well. I watched Joan's silent tears of good-bye, and managed my own sadness and frustration. I marveled at how far it seemed we had come together. I had moved beyond a naive understanding of the realities that Bobbie and Joan dealt with in their day-to-day lives, and it seemed that Joan had been given an experience of teacher as resource and ally.

WHAT IS A SOCIALLY JUST PRACTICE FOR GAY/LESBIAN FAMILIES?

Developmentally Appropriate Practice in Early Childhood Education Programs (Bredekamp & Copple, 1997) tells educators to make "professional" decisions based on "knowledge of the social and cultural contexts in which children live, to ensure that learning experiences are meaningful, relevant, and respectful of participation of children and their families" (p. 9). It insists that we build children's self-confidence, know each child well, build group cohesiveness, and bring the child's language and culture into the school. It dictates that we develop mutual relationships with families, listen carefully to what parents say about their children, attempt to understand parents' goals and preferences, and respect culture and family difference. There is, however, no specific reference to gay/lesbian-headed households in the book.

The series of position statements that constitute Bredekamp and Copple's (1997) book suggests that there is a wide interpretive range in the dominant discourse of early childhood education to acknowledge the complex family realities of children, which could include gay and lesbian families. However, with no specific recommendations or explicitly inclusive language, there is ambiguity about a teacher's responsibility to a child from a gay or lesbian family. The possibility exists that within an early childhood classroom, cultures of families will clash, parents' expressed desires for their children will differ significantly, and the gay/lesbian family will be shuffled under a cloak of silence and secrecy. Perhaps the gay/lesbian family is often subject to the vulnerabilities that Caleb's family faced. Caleb's parents chose to mask their identity in the school for realistic fear of public reprisal in their community. In so doing, they also rendered themselves invisible as a functional family unit to me (their child's first teacher) and others (their parent and teacher contemporaries).

In this narrative, decisions were negotiated in relation to cultural variables, wider community phenomena, personal comforts, schoolwide practices, and the individual needs of Caleb and his family. As a teacher, did I know who and what identities Bobbie and Joan wanted for themselves and their children? Did they need to get support from the school about their family, or was support for Caleb's family necessary for his emotional and social growth and development? Did Bobbie and Joan want the recognition that I thought they should have to legitimize their family? How did Caleb's parents give him information and coping skills about his lesbian family, and were these skills more effective than ones I could give Caleb as his teacher? Did I have to represent Caleb and his two parents in the symbolic forms of children's stories to legitimate their existence, *or* was I reinscribing heteronormative practices if I didn't? How would representing Caleb and his parents be achieved without school support in the form of inclusive policies? How did Phyllis and I together form a curriculum and act in ways that allowed Bobbie to come to our Open House? In what ways was this a socially just practice that neither of us could have done alone?

The ideas of representing Caleb's family to others in the school were eventually abandoned. Through the home and school relationship, I was informed of past homophobic prejudice in the community. I recognized the need for Caleb to have his family arrangement and relationship to Bobbie supported, and this superseded my desire to educate others about Caleb's family. My role as an educator in Caleb's case became one of fostering the positive relationship he already had with Bobbie. It entailed reflecting to Joan the valuable contributions they each made to their children's lives. While I felt constrained in representing visual images, and talking to the group as a whole about his lesbian family, I did not feel constraint in talking openly and honestly to Caleb personally. While the cultural constraints that I felt as a lesbian-identified teacher prohibited my use of visual images with Caleb and the other children, that was not the case for my heterosexual friend and co-teacher Phyllis.

The retelling of this story of teaching now suggests to me that representation and activism can take many forms that are contextually dependent. Bobbie's and Joan's open enjoyment and participation in the Open House affirmed for me that "dialectic" actions were as effective, if not more so, as "representational" ones (Morris, 1994). That is, our ongoing personal conversations and individually changed thought processes provided a strong framework for social action that was helpful in instigating social change. This approach seemed preferable over the approach of providing stories and images. This story of inclusion suggests that the world views (Adams, Bell, & Griffin, 1997) of participants in any transformational teaching event change externally as well as internally.

Inclusive school policies about gay/lesbian families can be developed proactively by groups of teachers, students, families, and administrators. Proactive philosophy development makes teachers less vulnerable. Classroom practice statements describe how inclusive philosophies are individually and socially appropriate and educate all parents about what types of discussions are likely to occur in the early childhood classroom.

Further, teachers can critically evaluate their understandings of gay and lesbian lifestyles, and evaluate the many ways in which their classrooms either foster or prohibit the inclusion of a gay/lesbian family. Gay and lesbian families who desire support from school personnel for their choices in parenting, relationships, and school involvement are likely to look for conversational and representational signs of inclusion. While gay/lesbian families may not always be conspicuous to teachers, inclusive (or exclusive) language, policy, and school activity are apparent to gay/lesbian families and will enhance (or diminish) school involvement.

Acknowledgment. Development of this chapter was supported by the professional development fund of the School of Education, University of Wisconsin–Madison, Spencer Research Training Program. The author expresses appreciation to the School and assumes responsibility for chapter content.

REFERENCES

Adams, M., Bell, L., & Griffin, P. (1997). *Teaching for diversity and social justice.* New York: Routledge.

Balster-Liontos, L. (1992). *At-risk families and schools: Becoming partners.* University of Oregon, College of Education.

Banks, J., & Banks, C. A. (Eds.). (1993). *Multi-cultural education: Issues and perspectives* (2nd ed.). Boston: Allyn & Bacon.

Bredekamp, S., & Copple, C. (1997). *Developmentally appropriate practice in early childhood education programs serving children from birth through age 8* (rev. ed.). Washington, DC: National Association for the Education of Young Children.

Brown McCracken, J. (1993). *Valuing diversity: The primary years.* Washington, DC: National Association for the Education of Young Children.

Casper, V., Cuffaro, H. K., Schultz, S., Silin, J. G., & Wickens, E. (1996). Toward a most thorough understanding of the world: Sexual orientation and early childhood education. *Harvard Educational Review, 66*(2), 271–293.

Casper, V., & Schultz, S. B. (1999). *Gay parents/straight schools: Building communication and trust.* New York: Teachers College Press.

Clay, J. (1990). Working with lesbian and gay parents and their children. *Young Children, 45*(2), 31–35.

Cordeiro, P., Reagan, T., & Martinez, L. (1994). *Multiculturalism and TOE: Addressing cultural diversity in schools.* Thousand Oaks, CA: Corwin.

Derman-Sparks, L. (1989). *Anti-bias curriculum: Tools for empowering young children.* Washington, DC: National Association for the Education of Young Children.

Epstein, J. L., Coates, L., Salinas, K. C., Sanders, M. G., & Simon, B. (1996). *Partnership 2000 schools manual: Improving school, family, community connections.* Baltimore: Johns Hopkins University, Center for Research on the Education of Students Placed at-Risk.

Fuller, M., & Olson, G. (1998). *Home–school relations: Working successfully with parents and families*. Boston: Allyn & Bacon.

Graue, M. E. (1993). Social networks and home–school relations. *Educational Policy, 7*(4), 466–490.

Graue, M. E., & Walsh, D. (1998). *Studying children in context: Theories, methods, and ethics*. Thousand Oaks, CA: Sage.

Hulsebosch, P., & Koerner, M. (1997). You can't be for children and against their families: Family diversity workshops for elementary school teachers. In J. Sears & W. Williams (Eds.), *Overcoming heterosexism and homophobia: Strategies that work*. New York: Columbia University Press.

Lareau, A., & Horvatt, M. (1999). Moments of social inclusion and exclusion: Race, class, and cultural capital in family–school relationships. *Sociology of Education, 72*(1), 37–53.

Miller-Lachmann, L., & Taylor, C. (1995). *Schools for all: Educating children in a diverse society*. Albany, NY: Delmar.

Morris, P. (1994). *The Bakhtin reader: Selected writings of Bakhtin, Medvedev, and Voloshnov*. London: Edward Arnold Hodder Headline PLC.

Neuman, L. (1989). *Heather has two mommies*. Boston: Alyson Wonderland.

Reglin, G. (1993). *At-risk "parent and family": School involvement strategies for low income families and African-American families of unmotivated and underachieving students*. Springfield, IL: Charles C. Thomas.

Sears, J. (1994). Challenges for educators: Lesbian, gay, and bisexual families. *The High School Journal, 77*, 138–155.

Silin, J. G. (1995). *Sex, death, and the education of children: Our passion for ignorance in the age of AIDS*. New York: Teachers College Press.

Sleeter, C., & Grant, C. (Eds.). (1994). *Making choices for multicultural education: Five approaches to race, class, and gender*. Columbus, OH: Merrill, Prentice-Hall.

Southern Poverty Law Center. (1997). *Starting small: Teaching tolerance in preschool and the early grades*. Birmingham, AL: Author.

Swap, S. (1993). *Developing home–school partnerships: From concepts to practice*. New York: Teachers College Press.

Warner, C. (1998). *Everybody's house—the schoolhouse: Best techniques for connecting home, school, and community*. Thousand Oaks, CA: Corwin.

PART III

Reconceptualized Identities: Expanding Cultural Representations

CHAPTER 6

Equity Observation and Images of Fairness in Childhood

Sheralyn Campbell & Kylie Smith

This is a time of suddenly acknowledged multiplicity and diversity. Voices long ignored or long repressed are making themselves heard, many of them demanding that we look at things from their perspectives and recognize how numerous are the ways of defining what is "real."

—Maxine Greene, "Gender, Multiplicity and Voice"

OUR INTEREST in observation is linked to our commitment to explore how our early childhood teaching practices are implicated in the way fairness operates in children's lives. We believe our understandings of childhood (and what it is to be a child) are constructed within a social, political, and historical context (Aries, 1962; Cleverly & Phillips, 1988; Dahlberg, Moss, & Pence, 1999; Genishi, Ryan, Ochsner, & Yarnall, in press; James, Jenks, & Prout, 1998; Silin, 1995). These understandings of childhood are discourses that focus our attention, assumptions, explanations, and actions within particular theoretical paradigms. In this way two observers may hold opposing images of a child because their competing discourses of childhood construct the way their gaze focuses on the child. Each observer may understand her truth as summative of the individual.

In this chapter we raise questions about how a traditional observation discourse acts to privilege and silence particular understandings of what it is to be a child in an early childhood setting. We suggest that the teacher's traditional gaze may have unintended effects for how fairness operates (and is opposed) in the everyday social world of a children's services center. We believe that reading observations from diverse philosophical positions can open disruptive spaces in which teachers may work to engage and change how fairness is part of children's lives.

TRADITIONAL DEVELOPMENT OBSERVATION

Observation of the individual child is understood as an essential component of good teaching in early childhood education (Almy & Genishi, 1979; Arthur, Beecher, Dockett, Farmer, & Death, 1996; Faragher & Mac Naughton, 1998; Katz & McClellan, 1997; Lambert, Clyde, & Reeves, 1987; Veale & Piscitelli, 1994). Martin (1994) summarized early childhood observation as "the informal or formal perception of behavior of an individual or group of people or the perceptions gained from looking at an environment or object" (p. 318).

Thus observation is a technique that the early childhood teacher uses to build an understanding of the early childhood setting and define who a child is within that setting. The early childhood teacher generally focuses her observation on a child's development across four main categories: cognitive, language, social/emotional, and physical (Almy & Genishi, 1979; Arthur, Beecher, Dockett, Farmer, & Death, 1996; Bergen, 1997; Bredekamp, 1987; Bredekamp & Copple, 1997; Bretherton, 1981; Cohen, Stern, & Balaban, 1997; Faragher & Mac Naughton, 1998). Using this focus, she appraises the child's development within broad socially and culturally defined norms and seeks dynamic individual differences to identify the child's needs and competencies (Katz, 1996). From observed fragments of a child's life, the teacher builds an image that defines the child as an individual. The early childhood literature suggests that the teacher can use this understanding of the individual to:

- Identify a child's strengths and weaknesses
- Monitor changes in development as they occur
- Evaluate or assess development and bring about change in a child's behavior
- Identify problems in learning and delays in development
- Inform parents about their child's development

- Build reports for other professionals in related disciplines (e.g., speech therapists or protective service workers)
- Design a curriculum that supports a child's development along a predetermined path to maturity (Almy & Genishi, 1979; Beaty, 1998; Bredekamp, 1987; Bretherton, 1981; Cohen, Stern, & Balaban, 1997; Faragher & Mac Naughton, 1998; Irwin & Bushnell, 1980; Lambert, Clyde, & Reeves, 1987; Medinnus, 1976; Veale & Piscitelli, 1994; Waters, 1999)

In our opinion, traditional observation contains two important epistemological assumptions about the abstract child that underpin understandings of the specific individual.

1. The child is akin to clay, made up of the essential developmental ingredients of her adulthood, but preformed. She has the freedom to progress toward the socially desirable shape and form of an independent, consistent, rational adult in her own unique way.
2. The teacher is the potter with the ability to know the child (from her theoretically informed, objective, and rational observations) and use this knowledge to correctly influence the shape and form that the child assumes.

The developmental image formed by traditional observation guides and informs the early childhood teacher's daily practice, predictions, interactions, interventions, and curriculum decisions.

Observation as Problematic

Michel Foucault (1977) examined the ways in which power is enacted within and through practices such as observation to discipline the individual as a social being. Further, he proposed that observation is neither value free nor objective, but inseparable from a teacher's theoretical knowledge that generally has defined the universal and normal child as developmental. This knowledge authorizes how teachers guide children's development in early childhood classrooms. Observation thus operates as a technique of power "aimed at extending the skills of the body . . . and reorganizing the body's forces . . . to foster a 'useful' obedience" (McHoul & Grace, 1997, p. 68). Because traditional observation values and privileges developmental forms of knowledge over other ways of knowing the child, the practice of observation acts as a disciplinary instrument of surveillance. The child's freedom to move toward adulthood is constrained by knowledge of what it is to be normal and desirable. The effect of privileging one form of knowledge (in this case, developmental knowledge) is to silence other complex social ways of knowing and being a boy or a girl. Hence the developmental image of the child becomes partial and apolitical—silencing meanings of race, class, culture, ability, age, and sexuality that operate within the daily life of the classroom. We believe teachers and children need to disrupt these silences in traditional observation images in order to contest and resist the effects of inequity and transform how fairness operates in the classroom.

We will explore our concerns about traditional observation using an episode of play called the construction site taken from an action research project in an inner-city Australian children's center. In 1997 and 1998, Sheralyn worked with a team of teachers and children reflecting on how equity operated in the 3- to 5-year-old classroom. In November 1997, she transcribed audio- and videotaped recordings of children playing in the construction site. Together the teachers (Kylie, Sandra, and Natalie) revisited the transcript and videotapes with Sheralyn. We looked at how our traditional developmental and feminist poststructural perspectives provided competing ways of reading play. Using the contrasts between these positions, we reflected on how equity operated for children.

The Construction Site Observation

The area was approximately 3 meters (10 feet) in width and 3 and a half meters (11.5 feet) long. One side of the area was made of large outdoor blocks stacked to child waist height. A pulley and large blue bucket hung from the ceiling almost in the center of the area. Props included large and small spades and scoops, hard hats, large witches' hats, wheelbarrows, a trolley, cardboard tubes, additional large blocks, and similar-sized cardboard boxes. The floor was covered with a one-inch layer of tanbark (woodchips). Sandra (the teacher and a research team member) worked nearby at a drawing table, which enabled her to become involved in the construction site if necessary.

In the play episode the participants include Rowena (3.11 years and Australian born), Mick (4.2 years and Sri Lankan born), and Helen (5.3 years and Jamaican born). Rowena, who is the only child in the construction site with English as a first language, has only recently begun attending the center.

BEGINNING PLAY

Rowena invites Mick to join her and then directs the play by telling him what to do and censoring some of his actions with, "No, Mick, not good!" She giggles and twirls her dress when he complies with her instructions.

HELEN'S ENTRY AND NEGOTIATIONS FOR BUILDING

HELEN: Am I allowed to play in here?
ROWENA: Yep.
HELEN (entering carefully): Look I have a skirt on today (spreading her skirt out wide).
ROWENA (spreading her dress in reply): And I have a dress on today (giggling).

Helen begins making a range of suggestions that include everyone in ongoing play. Rowena continues building with blocks and responds to each suggestion by giggling, ignoring Helen, agreeing to a suggestion (but not taking it up), talking loudly over Helen's words, or saying no.

BEFORE MICK'S FALL

Rowena continues to ignore Helen's suggestions, repeatedly dropping the pulley bucket onto Helen's stacked trolley of boxes, making it wobble. Mick watches some of the activity from astride a wheelbarrow near Rowena's feet. Helen offers another alternative for how to use the bucket in the game. Rowena excitedly agrees: "Yeah!" However, she pirouettes, letting the rope slip slowly through her hand, and the bucket falls once more onto Helen's trolley. Rowena leans on the block wall and looks at Mick. She sighs and rolls her eyes to the ceiling. Mick laughs and rocks side to side on the wheelbarrow without falling. Rowena stacks boxes on the wall, ignoring Helen, who leaves her trolley and, with her eyes downcast, moves toward Rowena and Mick.

MICK'S FALL

Helen bends, scooping tanbark: "It's not funny" (low voice). Mick looks at Helen and rocks the wheelbarrow sideways. He falls slowly onto her pile of tanbark—bumping some of the wall blocks. Rowena turns and looks at Mick, who appears unhurt. He smiles up at Helen, who stands without moving.

SANDRA'S HELP

SANDRA (moving quickly into the area): Are you OK Mick? Do
  you want a hand?
(Mick says nothing and continues lying on the floor.)
ROWENA: Mick knocked the blocks down!
SANDRA: That's OK, he actually fell down. Rowena, we can actu-
  ally build it up.

Sandra stacks the blocks back up while Helen and Rowena stand
silently. When Sandra leaves, Mick sits on the wheelbarrow
again.

PLAY CONTINUES

HELEN (in a low voice): That's what I was telling you, Rowena.
  Some one will, will . . .
(As Helen speaks Mick begins to rock on the barrow again as if
  he might fall.)
HELEN: Don't Mick, you might hurt yourself. Mick it's not funny
  and you might hurt yourself and you might cry. (Helen
  walks back to the trolley and boxes.)

INTERPRETING THE OBSERVATION FROM DIVERSE PERSPECTIVES

We will now use both traditional developmental and feminist poststructural perspectives to make sense of the construction site observation. These contrasting narratives construct different views of the children involved, different interpretations of the interactions, and
different possibilities for how Sandra, the teacher, could work with
the children.

A Traditional Developmental Interpretation

In our first discussion of the construction site observation, a developmental interpretation emerged. Sandra described how the consistent
images she held of each child enabled her to understand Mick's fall as
unskilled and accidental. Her image of each child framed her understanding of what happened among the children in play and structured
the intent of her actions when she intervened. As a teacher committed
to gender equity and fairness, she wanted to ensure that the children's
exploration of nontraditional and collaborative gender roles in dra-
matic play was not diverted by their different abilities. She saw herself

as a model, guide, mediator, and scaffolder of individual learning. Sandra believed that promoting fairness in play required her to build each child's level of rational thinking and social language. Sandra's developmental image of each child and her interpretation within the observation follow:

Mick was the silent watcher who wanted to be included in play with other children but lacked the necessary interpretive and expressive language skills (in English, his second language). He was physically uncoordinated and socially vulnerable. Mick was unable to understand the complexity of the social negotiations that Helen and Rowena were attempting. He needed Sandra to decode, verbalize, and explain his fall for others so he would continue to be included in the play.

Rowena was a focused builder in her play. She lacked authority within the group because she was the youngest and newest member, and was still at the associative rather than cooperative level in her social interactions. Rowena's group status and socially egocentric play style meant she was unable to engage in equally collaborative play at Helen's level or, when Mick fell, to show concern for his welfare—or Helen's interrupted play. She needed Sandra as a model and scaffolder of more advanced social skills in order to be able to continue to focus on her learning with minimal interruption or conflict.

Helen was a "substitute teacher" in the early childhood classroom. As a capable, cognitively and linguistically skilled social negotiator (in English, her second language), she had reasoning and social skills that made her a valuable and "adult-like" learning resource to others. She was able to verbally challenge and resist unfairness, adjust her play to recognize and make allowances for differences in others, or ask for help from adults if necessary. Helen wanted to be part of the group in the construction site. She recognized the different abilities of her co-players in her attempts to find ways for everyone to play together. She didn't need Sandra's assistance when Mick fell, or in ongoing play, because she had correctly interpreted the accident. Helen's silence was intended to encourage and include Mick in ongoing play. Helen had the social skills necessary to continue play when Sandra left, and Sandra could rely on Helen's concern for the welfare of her co-players and her maturity as a model and facilitator of their learning.

A Feminist Poststructuralist Reading

Feminist poststructuralism offers a critique of the interpretation of individuals as rational and consistent (Burman, 1994; Henriques, Holloway, Urwin, Venn, & Walkerdine, 1984; Morss, 1996; Walkerdine,

1984; Weedon, 1997). In this critique, the way in which the child understands herself is viewed as shifting and changing as she accesses and invests in different socially, politically, and historically constructed meanings (Davies, 1989, 1993; Mac Naughton, 1995). By thinking about how each child accessed and invested in competing ways of being a boy or a girl (or subject positions)—and how these subject positions limited and made possible what each child could think, say, and do—we began to create a different story about how power operated to make it possible to be included in play (Davies, 1993; Mac Naughton, 1995, 1996, 1998). By adding our voices and a critical feminist image to Sandra's narrative, we saw children engaged in a constant struggle to define and redefine themselves within (and through) competing (and contradictory) discourses in circulation— some of which were more powerful than others (Alloway, 1995; Davies, 1993; Mac Naughton, 1995, 1996, 1998; Walkerdine & the Girls and Mathematics Unit, 1989; Weedon, 1997). This made the constant image of the children that emerged from our traditional developmental interpretation problematic. Rather, we saw children involved in contextually shifting processes of recognizing, desiring, imagining, accessing, emotionally investing in, practicing, and resisting the multiple ways of being a girl (or boy) that operated in the construction site.

Our feminist poststructuralist interpretation (a second reading) of the observation revealed how images of Mick and Rowena as developmentally noncognizant and unskilled meant that other important aspects of play were not seen, including:

- How Rowena was able to silence and marginalize Helen's attempts at inclusion by using the language and practices of a nonreasoning, but desirable, girl
- How Rowena was able to use mockery to trivialize the impact of her actions on Helen's play
- How Mick's laughter and fall colluded with Rowena's exclusions of Helen, preventing her from persisting in her attempts to contribute to the story lines that were valued in play
- How Mick was able to threaten further physical interventions when Helen continued her reasoned approaches
- How Sandra's intervention endorsed and trivialized the unfairness being perpetrated by Mick's and Rowena's actions ("That's OK, he actually fell down")

Together, Mick and Rowena used language and practices that constituted particular ways of being a "boy" and a "girl." Rowena spoke as a nonreasoning, but desirable, White female; Mick spoke as the desiring and potent protective male. Their communications represented a form of patriarchal discourse. Helen used a competing rationalist discourse, speaking as a rational and reasoning Black female. This was a discourse that Sandra valued and recognized as empowering.

Sandra's continuous traditional image of the children as people who fit particular developmental characteristics prevented her from seeing how competing discourses shifted the terrain of power, limiting the possibilities for who each child could be. For example, Rowena and Mick's and patriarchal discourse worked against Helen's rational discourse. In their collusions, Helen was regulated, marginalized, and silenced. Mick's investments in the patriarchal discourse included him in play in ways that Sandra's traditional developmental images did not reveal or dispute. Further, the children constructed Sandra's understandings even as she constructed the meanings of their play. For example, Helen could have spoken to Sandra about the unfairness; however, to do so would have positioned her outside the patriarchal discourse the children were using, risking further exclusion from play. There was also an added risk that bringing her unsuccessful negotiations to Sandra's attention might reposition her as "child" rather than "adult-like" in Sandra's discourse. Because Sandra's intervention did not problematize how power was operating within and through competing discourses to make some ways of being a boy or a girl more desirable, pleasurable, and possible, a racist and sexist status quo was continued by the children and by Sandra. The traditional images constructed by developmental observation failed to contest the equity politics of what it was to be a boy or a girl in the construction site and how those politics limited the individual participants.

PROBLEMS AND POSSIBILITIES: INTERPRETING OBSERVATIONS

Sandra's teaching for equity within traditional perspectives was limited to providing a developmentally suitable environment and guiding children toward rational thinking and social collaboration. Her traditional teaching practice was unable to contest the contradictions in how fairness was enacted in children's relationships because these did not fit within the developmental images of each child.

Two assumptions contributed to the ineffectiveness of Sandra's traditional discourse for critically engaging and transforming equity relations:

1. *Teachers were viewed as knowledgeable and insightful agents in the classroom situation.* Traditional observation assumed

that Sandra was able to put together a true picture of each who each child was as an individual—her or his transcendental true self. The correctness of the image of the child built over many contacts and developmental records guaranteed that Sandra's intentions and actions would guide each child in her or his journey toward becoming an autonomous, rational being. Hence, the children's abilities as human agents to resist and politically subvert Sandra's teaching to their own ends went unrecognized.

2. *Rationality was accepted as the key to freedom and agency.* Traditional observation situated each child as a fixed and continuous individual whose identity was played out across different situations in the same way. Each child was constituted as able to freely choose between the possibilities for being a boy or a girl in the construction site. Their choices were viewed as limited by their own individual cognitive and social abilities rather than by broader discursive practices in the classroom and the specific play situation. Hence, contextually shifting relations of power–knowledge that made some ways of being a boy or a girl more desirable, possible, and pleasurable remained unrecognized and unchallenged.

Surveillance, Normalization, and Discipline

Traditional observation created developmental images of each child that became a form of surveillance. The consistent images formed uncontested frames that were applied apolitically to how Sandra understood what happened in play and relationships in the construction site. Sandra's actions became a form of normalization and reproduced the status quo in social relationships by silencing other powerful aspects of how children understood themselves and others. Developmental images served the interests of adult/child separations and patriarchy. Sandra's traditional observation and developmental images worked against her aspirations for gender equity and fairness.

Shifting the Terrain of Observation to Images of Fairness

We believe as teachers that using both developmental and feminist poststructural perspectives to undertake multiple readings of our observations is one way of making these hidden assumptions, silences, and contradictory effects visible. Multiple readings make visible the way in which particular discourses act to constrain and limit what is possible, desirable, and pleasurable for children in their play and relationships. The use of multiple perspectives replaces the certainty of traditional observational readings of the child with competing understandings and voices that are questioning, uncertain, relative, and complex.

As we explored additional possibilities through two readings of the same situation, we recognized that our understandings of ourselves and others are indivisible from the social location of the people and institutions that constitute our theory and practice. Multiple readings of the same observation enabled us to increase possibilities for equity and fairness by including questions like the following:

- Who has the right to observe? Who has been excluded? How is observation designed so that many voices and perspectives are included?
- Who and what is observed? How do we fairly broaden our gaze to look at the complexity of who we are as social beings within a political, cultural, and historical context? How have children been included or excluded in this complex gaze?
- How are observations recorded and documented? What methods of observing offer opportunities to read, reread, and challenge our understandings?
- Does observation operate as a practice of equity and fairness? Whose interests are served by our observations and what are the political implications and material effects of privileging these ways of knowing? (Campbell, 1999; Smith, 2000)

Teachers and researchers will need to explore ways of viewing children and classroom activities from multiple perspectives. Examples could involve paired observations and discussion, the use of multiple theoretical discourses to understand events, and the exploration of diverse perspectives on equity and fairness in classroom activities. Specific suggestions include the following:

1. *Compare subjectivities in observation.* With another teacher, observe children at play. Simultaneously write what you see and record the observation on videotape. Critically examine the differences between what each person wrote and what is on tape. What personal and professional knowledge has enabled each person to record, see, and understand the play in a particular way? What personal and professional investments does

each person have in the different ways of seeing and understanding play?

2. *Use two different theoretical discourses to focus and make
   sense of an observation.* What does each theoretical discourse
   allow you to talk about and do? What is discussed? What is
   silent or left out? In whose interests do these theoretical discourses operate? What are the political and material implications of these discourses and silences for your teaching?

3. *Create a method of observation that you believe will work for
   fairness from you and between children.* What are the specific
   issues of equity that you believe must be included? How does
   your process respond to these issues? Share this method with
   a teacher from a different cultural background, asking her or
   him to decide what has been "left out."

As teachers, we believe that working with others for a better world
requires us to critically examine our taken-for-granted teaching knowledge, language, and practices. Our attempts include trying to rethink
our observational practices as practices that work for equity and fairness.

REFERENCES

Alloway, N. (1995). *Foundation stones: The construction of gender in early
    childhood.* Carlton, Victoria: Curriculum Corporation.

Almy, M., & Genishi, C. (1979). *Ways of studying children.* New York: Teach-
    ers College Press.

Aries, P. (1962). *Centuries of childhood: A social history of family life.* New
    York: Vintage Books.

Arthur, L., Beecher, B., Dockett, S., Farmer, S., & Death, E. (1996). *Program-
    ming and planning in early childhood settings* (2nd ed.). Sydney: Har-
    court Brace.

Beaty, J. (1998). *Observing development of the young child* (4th ed.). Engle-
    wood Cliffs, NJ: Prentice-Hall.

Bergen, D. (1997). Using observational techniques for evaluating young chil-
    dren's learning. In B. Spodek & O. Saracho (Eds.), *Yearbook of early
    childhood education: Vol. 7. Issues in early childhood educational as-
    sessment and evaluation* (pp. 108–128). New York: Teachers College
    Press.

Bredekamp, S. (Ed.). (1987). *Developmentally appropriate practice in early
    childhood programs serving children from birth through age 8.* Washing-
    ton, DC: National Association for the Education of Young Children.

Bredekamp, S., & Copple, C. (1997). *Developmentally appropriate practice in early childhood programs serving children from birth through age 8* (rev. ed.). Washington, DC: National Association for the Education of Young Children.

Bretherton, D. (1981). *A system for keeping individual records in the Piagetian pre-school program*. Melbourne: Institute of Early Childhood Development.

Burman, E. (1994). *Deconstructing developmental psychology*. London: Routledge.

Campbell, S. (1999). Making the political pedagogical in early childhood education. *Australian Journal of Early Childhood, 24*(4), 21–26.

Cleverly, J., & Phillips, D. (1988). *Visions of childhood: Influential models from Locke to Spock*. Sydney: Allen & Unwin.

Cohen, D., Stern, V., & Balaban, N. (1997). *Observing and recording the behavior of young children* (4th ed.). New York: Teachers College Press.

Dahlberg, G., Moss, P., & Pence, A. (1999). *Beyond quality in early childhood education and care: Postmodern perspectives*. London: Falmer Press.

Davies, B. (1989). *Frogs and snails and feminist tales: Preschool children and gender*. North Sydney, NSW: Allen & Unwin.

Davies, B. (1993). *Shards of glass: Children reading and writing beyond gendered identities*. North Sydney, NSW: Allen & Unwin.

Faragher, J., & Mac Naughton, G. (1998). *Working with young children: Guidelines for good practice* (2nd ed.). Melbourne: RMIT Publishing.

Foucault, M. (1977). *Discipline and punish: The birth of the prison system* (A. Sheridan, Trans.). Harmondsworth, England: Penguin.

Genishi, C., Ryan, S., Ochsner, M., & Yarnall, M. M. (in press). Teaching in early childhood education: Understanding practices through research and theory. In V. Richardson (Ed.), *Handbook of research on teaching* (4th ed.). Washington, DC: American Educational Research Association.

Greene, M. (1993). Gender, multiplicity and voice. In S. Biklen & D. Pollard (Eds.), *Gender and education* (pp. 241–256). Chicago: National Society for the Study of Education.

Henriques, J., Holloway, W., Urwin, C., Venn, C., & Walkerdine, V. (1984). Introduction to section 2: Constructing the subject. In J. Henriques, W. Holloway, C. Urwin, C. Venn, & V. Walkerdine (Eds.), *Changing the subject: Psychology, social regulation and subjectivity* (pp. 91–118). London: Methuen.

Irwin, D. M., & Bushnell, M. M. (1980). *Observational strategies for child study*. New York: Holt, Rinehart & Winston.

James, A., Jenks, C., & Prout, A. (1998). *Theorizing childhood*. New York: Teachers College Press.

Katz, L. G. (1996). Children as learners: A developmental approach. In *Proceedings of the Weaving Webs Conference*. Melbourne University, Department of Early Childhood Studies, Melbourne.

Katz, L. G., & McClellan, D. E. (1997). *Fostering children's social competence:*

The teacher's role. Washington, DC: National Association for the Education of Young Children.

Lambert, B., Clyde, M., & Reeves, K. (1987). *Planning for individual needs in early childhood services.* Watson, ACT: Australian Early Childhood Association.

Mac Naughton, G. (1995). A post structuralist analysis of learning in early childhood settings. In M. Fleer (Ed.), *DAPcentrism: Challenging developmentally appropriate practice* (pp. 35– 54). Watson, ACT: Australian Early Childhood Association.

Mac Naughton, G. (1996). The gender factor. In B. Creaser & E. Dau (Eds.), *The anti-bias approach in early childhood* (pp. 51–70). Sydney: Harper Educational.

Mac Naughton, G. (1998). Improving our gender equity tools: A case for discourse analysis. In N. Yelland (Ed.), *Gender in early childhood* (pp. 149–174). London: Routledge.

Martin, S. (1994). *Take a look: Observation and portfolio assessment in early childhood.* Don Mills, ON: Addison-Wesley.

McHoul, A., & Grace, W. (1997). *A Foucault primer: Discourse, power and the subject.* Melbourne: Melbourne University Press.

Medinnus, G. R. (1976). *Child study and observation guide.* New York: Wiley.

Morss, J. R. (1996). *Growing critical: Alternatives to developmental psychology.* London: Routledge.

Silin, J. G. (1995). *Sex, death, and the education of children: Our passion for ignorance in the age of AIDS.* New York: Teachers College Press.

Smith, K. (2000). Reconceptualising the role of parents in observation. *Australian Journal of Early Childhood, 25*(2), 18–21.

Veale, A., & Piscitelli, B. (1994). *Observation and record keeping in early childhood programs.* Watson, ACT: Australian Early Childhood Association.

Walkerdine, V. (1984). Developmental psychology and the child centered pedagogy: The insertion of Piaget into early childhood education. In J. Henriques, W. Holloway, C. Urwin, C. Venn, & V. Walkerdine (Eds.), *Changing the subject: Psychology, social regulation and subjectivity* (pp. 153–202). London: Methuen.

Walkerdine, V., & the Girls and Mathematics Unit. (1989). *Counting girls out.* London: Virago.

Waters, J. (1999). *Observation: A window to the child.* Melbourne: National Gowrie/RAP Consortium.

Weedon, C. (1997). *Feminist practice and poststructuralist theory* (2nd ed.). Oxford: Basil Blackwell.

CHAPTER 7

A Messy Closet in the Early Childhood Classroom

Rachel Theilheimer & Betsy Cahill

CLASSROOMS FOR young children are supposed to have well-organized closets. Yet, we are finding a messy virtual or metaphorical closet in the field of early childhood. In it is a jumble of myths, beliefs, norms, and representations of sexuality and children that spill out into the room, affecting how teachers and children see themselves and others. In an effort to open the door and clean the closet, this chapter investigates ignorances, assumptions, and silences about sexuality, using stories from our own experiences.

IGNORANCES, ASSUMPTIONS, AND SILENCES

If talk of sexuality in general is "problematic and even potentially dangerous" (Tobin, 1997, p. 1) in the early childhood classroom, introducing possibilities of sexual orientation is even riskier. Early childhood education has taken what Sedgwick (1990) calls the minoritizing view, regarding sexual orientation as of importance to only a few and keeping the issue of sexual orientation under cover. Yet, according to Sedgwick, "the relations of the closet—the relations of the known and the unknown, the explicit and the inexplicit around homo/heterosexual definition—have the potential for being peculiarly revealing" (p. 3). Our ignorances, silences, and assumptions about gay, lesbian, and bisexual possibilities in the early childhood classroom are surely, in Sedgwick's words, "as pointed and performative as speech" and "as potent and as multiple a thing there as is knowledge" (p. 4).

The researchers, policy makers, practitioners, and teacher educators in early childhood education generally ignore children's eventually emerging sexuality. We use "eventually emerging sexuality" to differentiate between the behavior and "psychic core" (Butler, 1996, p. 60) that identify adults' sexualities, and children's perhaps unobservable, but evolving, affectional preferences and sexual orientations. The adult's sense of sexual self resides in a culturally created category that situates sexual fantasies, attractions, and behaviors (Savin-Williams, 1995). While most of children's sexual behaviors differ from adults', children actively construct "their own understandings [in this case, of sexuality] . . . mediated by and clearly linked to the sociocultural context" (Bredekamp & Copple, 1997, p. 13). In this chapter we try not to attribute adult sexual behavior to children, but to acknowledge the influence of early childhood experiences on children's attitudes toward their own and other children's eventually emerging sexualities.

Many children are learning about their sexual selves in local and broader contexts that assume that everyone is heterosexual until proven otherwise. In the discussion that follows, we interrogate this assumption of heteronormativity (heterosexuality as the normal) in a variety of situations.

On Romance, Flirtation, and the Teacher's Closet

Homophobia is "prejudice, discrimination, harassment, or acts of violence against sexual minorities . . . evidenced in a deep-seated fear or hatred of those who love and sexually desire those of the same sex" (Sears, 1997, p. 16). In early childhood classrooms, homophobia may not demonstrate itself as visible discrimination, harassment, or violence, yet prejudice may be manifest when teachers ignore possibilities that are not heterosexual.

Sears (1997) cites Gregory Herek (1990), who differentiates between "cultural heterosexism [that] is a stigmatization, denial, or denigration of non-heterosexuality in cultural institutions" and "psychological heterosexism [that] is a person's internalization of this world view, which erupts into antigay prejudice" (p. 16). Our goal is to help teachers make their classrooms cultural institutions where there is not stigmatization, denial, or denigration of nonheterosexuality and that help children internalize repugnance for prejudice and bias.

Going into early childhood classrooms, one does not readily observe teachers' fear of or prejudice against gay, lesbian, or bisexual individuals. Yet, as Cahill (1995) found, early childhood teachers do have homophobic beliefs. Since children frequently are represented as innocent and asexual (Cannella, 1997; Silin, 1995) and since teachers tend to avoid sexuality in general (Tobin, 1997), it is not surprising that homophobia is not evinced toward children in easily discernible ways. Yet children *are* regarded as sexual beings by adults, at least some of the time, and this imputed sexuality tends to be heterosexual. One easily enough finds images of a little boy and little girl romantically paired in advertisements and commercials.

Even without explicit sexual imagery, heteronormativity—the pervasive assumption that all children and adolescents are heterosexual—is evident, and children's photos are only one of its media. Heteronormativity pervades early childhood classrooms as well. An early childhood education student, in an observation of a child, caught herself short:

> He seemed to be particularly close to a girl I will call Lisa. I had to laugh at myself when I realized that my initial thoughts about their relationship were romantic in nature. A moment later, remembering what it was like to be a kid, it occurred to me that it was entirely likely that Lisa was simply his "best friend" for that day.

By re-evaluating her assumption of romantic interest, the student refrained from imposing adult intentions on a child. In this writing, however, she did not probe the implicit heteronormativity.

Another student wrote in an observation that a 6-year-old boy looked at her flirtatiously. Would this female student have attributed flirtation to a girl who looked at her in the same way? What about a female child and a male teacher? Would that raise additional questions or concerns for us? Would a male child seem flirtatious to a male teacher? Why or why not? This student's simple observation raises questions about sex-role stereotypes, heteronormative assumptions, and beliefs about sexual deviance and intergenerational sex (Rubin, 1984).

In both of these writings students seemed not to question a norm of heterosexuality. They at least briefly regarded these children as sexual beings, attributing heterosexual behavior to them. These students' representations of children, interpretations, and subsequent practices could reinforce heteronormativity for children who will be and will not be gay.

Heteronormative representations underlie more overt heterosexist practices. When teachers talk as if young children had boyfriends and girlfriends of the opposite sex, for example, they give implicit heteronormative messages. From these messages and from more direct information, children learn that heterosexuality is expected eventual behavior. When teachers narrowly define families or do not intervene when children use epithets such as faggot, children learn about both norms and prejudice. These practices can limit the development of a positive identity based on an acceptance and integration of one's sexual identities (Savin-Williams, 1995). Heteronormativity can lay the groundwork of "the twin plagues" (Sears, 1997, p. 14) of homophobia and heterosexism for all children.

Bert and Ernie in the Closet

Denial can lead to subtle stigmatization or blatant denigration. Are Bert and Ernie gay? At a workshop on gay and lesbian issues in the early childhood classroom, we learned that this question had been posed to the Children's Television Workshop (CTW). CTW's response: What do you mean? They're muppets! An inanimate object can't be gay. Muppets have only the sexual identity awarded them by their makers. Yet, CTW's response to the question ignores the meaning some children (and adults) might construct based on Bert and Ernie's behavior. Here are two males who share their home and care deeply about each other. Might they not be gay?

We are reminded of our own experiences. A parent worries that his son's dress-up play will make him gay. In a variety of ways, the child-care provider reassures the parent that his child's behavior will not cause homosexuality. This reassurance, as did CTW's denials, avoids admitting the possibility of being gay. Without forthrightly addressing the fear of a child's (or muppet's) potential to be gay, lesbian, or bisexual, the homophobia remains closeted, undiscussed, and implicitly unquestioned. About 20 years ago, Pogrebin (1980) offered an alternative: Her advice to parents was, "Don't worry about how to raise a heterosexual child; worry about how not to be a homophobic parent" (p. 292). Since the family and the media are among the "primary producers of sexual ideology" (Rubin, 1984, p. 294), parents and teachers must examine underlying homophobia to avoid passing dangerously biased meanings to children through ignorance, silence, or more blatant behaviors.

In a study of suburban middle-class attitudes (Wolfe, 1998), in-depth interviews with 200 people revealed surprising tolerance for and acceptance of differences, with one exception. While Wolfe's respondents avoided blatant expressions of racism, they did not eschew words such as abnormal, unacceptable, mentally deficient, sick, and untrustworthy to describe homosexuals. Wolfe's study suggests widespread acceptance of prejudice against and denigration of lesbian, gay, and bisexual individuals.

Early childhood policy makers also have not treated prejudice against gays, lesbians, and bisexuals in the same way as racism, sexism, handicappism, and other biases. The National Association for the Education of Young Children (NAEYC) has used the anti-bias curriculum (Derman-Sparks, 1989) to set a standard for the early childhood profession. The curriculum guide states:

> Some adults fear that encouraging nontraditional gender behavior leads to homosexuality (boys who play with dolls, or who cry; girls who prefer large-motor activities or don't like to wear dresses). This is a reflection of the deep homophobia in our society. There is no research evidence that nontraditional gender behavior creates homosexuality. Nevertheless, teachers may need to spend time in educational discussions with parents who are frightened by their children participating in certain activities, and may have to make choices about what activities they will stand up for and which they will modify or let go. (p. 54)

Throughout, the curriculum recommends offering information, negotiating ideas, and creating safe settings for discussions and collaborative curriculum development with families. If, after valiant efforts, parents and teachers cannot agree, teachers are instructed by the guide to hold firm to their anti-bias position, except in the specific instances of homophobia and heterosexism.

We recognize the historical context in which the anti-bias curriculum is situated. It has moved the field of early childhood education forward for the past decade. Throughout this time, NAEYC has issued position statements and published articles (Casper, Cuffaro, Schultz, Silin, & Wickens, 1996; Clay, 1990; Corbett, 1993; Wickens, 1993), even asking its membership to think about children's eventually emerging sexualities (Cahill & Theilheimer, 1999). Despite these strides, there is work to be done. As Audre Lorde (1983) reminds us:

> If we truly intend to eliminate oppression and achieve human liberation, heterosexism and homophobia must be addressed. As in the struggle against racism and sexism, courage, commitment and integrity are required. (p. 9)

Research in/on the Closet

Research on children's sexuality is not in most child development textbooks. We looked at the child development and introductory early childhood texts on our shelves. We found that when sexuality was listed in the indices of these texts, it referred us only to sections on sex roles, Freudian identity theories, sexual abuse, and talking to children about reproduction. Sexuality in general and homosexuality in specific remain in the closet in many early childhood education textbooks.

Although sexual functioning in adulthood has its origins in childhood (Lively & Lively, 1991), North American culture is largely ignorant and neglectful of young children's sexual development. Why, if sexuality has its roots in childhood, is the literature so silent about early childhood sexual development? According to Lewis (1987), human sexuality has received almost no attention in the child development literature because prior to puberty the constructs of sexual attraction and choice of sexual partner cannot be studied. The dearth of empirical research on children's developing sexuality is linked to assumptions that children are not sexual beings, perhaps confusing sexual behavior with identity (Savin-Williams, 1995).

In fact, there are no consistent findings in the literature on how a child develops a heterosexual, homosexual, or bisexual orientation. Sexual orientation appears to be formed by a complex interplay of psychological, biological, and social situations (Strickland, 1995). Categories such as heterosexual, homosexual, or bisexual help people make sense of the world, but are socially constructed and shift over time and depend on place and culture. The categories of sexual behaviors have particularly fuzzy boundaries and overlapping terrain (Mondimore, 1996). These culturally created categories of sexuality—defined by twentieth-century, adult Europeans and Americans—may hold little meaning for children.

According to Clausen (1997), "Everybody's sexuality comes from somewhere; to know what it is to be sexual, one must draw on systems of shared public meaning" (p. 49). With sexuality in the closet in early childhood classrooms, the systems of shared public meaning are present, but obscured. More research is needed to understand what homosexuality, bisexuality, and heterosexuality mean to young children and how that meaning affects their present and future beliefs, feelings, and actions. We do not know at what age and how children develop their sexual orientation, and we are not certain that is the germane question. We can be sure, however, that young children are developing images of themselves that influence their understandings and acceptance of their own and others' sexualities. This issue is at the core of the missing research.

BREAKING THE SILENCE

Members of professional organizations have been thinking critically about heterosexism and how to intervene effectively against it. The National Education Association, Association for Supervision and Curriculum Development (Goodman, 1993), National Association for the Education of Young Children, and accreditation agencies including the National Council for the Accreditation of Teacher Education have "encouraged the integration of content relating to lesbian and gay issues in the professional curriculum" (Sears, 1997, p. 14). Yet the content has not become a part of the everyday of teacher education.

We search for ways to make gay, lesbian, and bisexual issues for children, families, and teachers a part of our classes. Discussions related to sexuality sometimes discomfit early childhood education students (King, 1997), as we know for ourselves from course evaluations. Yet students raised the topic themselves when the Rainbow Curriculum, including suggestions for teaching about gay and lesbian families and other family constellations, was proposed for the New York City public schools. With the "Love Makes a Family" exhibit at the campus museum, a trip for the family–school–community collaboration class was an obvious fit. Still, one student in a colleague's social studies methods course resisted going into the exhibit, demanding to know whether her grade hinged upon her participation. Sometimes students resist our introduction of these issues; other times they raise them. We regard breaking the silence as the instructor's responsibility.

Can We Open the Closet Door?

Sears (1997) cautions that when sexuality issues emerge from the teacher education closet, "teaching techniques generally fail to move from the psychology of the other to the phenomenology of self" (p. 26). Teaching strategies such as role plays and reflective journals can have impacts as educational interventions because they ask students who are "uninformed heterosexist[s]" (p. 27) to take a position other than their own and provide vehicles for discussion. Changing attitudes is not enough; behavior must change as well, and teaching strategies must help teacher educators and their students consider how to do that. Toward this end, all of us can confront and address internalized heterosexist world views.

For us, this project is easier for the ally, who has less to risk professionally than the gay, lesbian, or bisexual teacher educator who fears exposure, its repercussions, and invasion of privacy. What Sedgwick (1990) calls "the deadly elasticity of heterosexist presumption" (p. 68) places the gay, lesbian, or bisexual educator in the position of never-ending decision maker about coming out. The danger inherent in coming out in some academic situations (Tierney, 1997) interferes with what we know to be the power that personal relationships can wield in helping students and colleagues overcome prejudice (Williams, 1997).

Is the Closet Door Already Open?

According to Silin, "Popular cultural images of young children as innocent . . . are often linked with ideas about childhood ignorance. Teachers and parents want to protect children from knowledge of the social world that they themselves find discomforting" (Casper et al., 1996, pp. 290–291). However, early childhood educators have underestimated what children figure out, know, and can understand about gay and lesbian relationships (Casper & Schultz, 1999; King, 1997). Children construct their own understandings of relationships. They bring what they know about the world into early childhood classrooms. They ask questions about our partners and family relationships and about who can marry whom (Cahill & Theilheimer, 1999). A personal story illustrates how knowledgeable children are and how illuminating it is to check to see what they understand. On the day that one of the children brought in *It's Christmas Eve, Bear*, the coordinators of student teaching at the local university were visiting to see whether the school was good enough to place student teachers. The teacher chose to read the book aloud to reinforce the child's interest in books and make the home–school connection. As she read, "it's Christmas Eve, Bear," a phrase repeated in the book, 5-year-old Bobby blurted out gleefully, "Eve, Eve, that's your wife's name!" His teacher's partner, Eve, had been to school often to build bookshelves. The lesbian teacher did not know what to do. With the authorities watching, she corrected him, saying, "Oh, you must mean my dear friend, Eve."

Bobby knew Eve and his teacher went places together, cooked food for each other, and lived together, just as his parents did. Bobby had constructed his own understanding of his teacher's relationship with Eve, although he had not been told directly about it. Bobby's teacher worried that his connection making during storytime revealed that she was a lesbian, perhaps jeopardizing her own and her school's standing with university authorities.

Here is an instance in which a practitioner did not validate a child's perception about a lesbian family. While she steered away from the topic for a possibly well-founded fear of exposure, others stay away because in their minds such references are linked to sex. By contrast, most people do not consider references to opposite-sex relationships—about mothers and fathers, for example—to be related to sex at all.

Whether to shield children from sexual content or to protect themselves, adults may try to hide information that children take for granted. This makes ignorance, closets, and the heteronormativity of the early childhood classroom all the more poignant.

CLASSROOM POSSIBILITIES

Five-year-old Chloe was thrilled when she was told that her mother's friends were lesbians who lived together. Now, it seemed to Chloe that she and her best friend could be together forever. Will Chloe grow up to be a lesbian? We do not know. Will she take heterosexuality for granted? Probably less than she would have, had her environment been more constricted. We cannot know the effect of her exposure to a lesbian couple and her mother's friendship with them. We—teacher educators and our students—*can* observe and talk to her and other children to understand how they conceptualize their social world in relation to their eventually emerging sexual selves.

The early childhood classroom still has a messy closet. Early childhood educators must open the door to that closet and take myths, beliefs, and norms off the shelves, examine them, and discard damaging ones. If early childhood teacher educators join students in scrutinizing the relationships between what we know and do not know and between what we articulate and remain silent about, we will learn more about ourselves. The children are an invaluable source of information, as they tell us what they know and understand. In this process, instructors and their students will reshelve some beliefs, because not everything we think we know about sexuality will become part of everyday classroom life. Other beliefs will come out in the classroom, where they have not been used before.

REFERENCES

Bredekamp, S., & Copple, C. (1997). *Developmentally appropriate practice in early childhood education programs serving children from birth through age 8* (rev. ed.). Washington, DC: National Association for the Education of Young Children.

Butler, J. (1996). Sexual inversions. In S. J. Hekman (Ed.), *Feminist interpretations of Michel Foucault* (pp. 59–75). University Park: Pennsylvania State University Press.

Cahill, B. (1995). *An exploratory study of early childhood teachers' attitudes toward gender roles.* Unpublished doctoral dissertation, Kent State University, Kent, OH.

Cahill, B., & Theilheimer, R. (1999). Can Tommy and Sam get married? Questions about gender, sexuality, and children. *Young Children, 54*(1), 27–31.

Cannella, G. S. (1997). *Deconstructing early childhood education: Social justice and revolution.* New York: Peter Lang.

Casper, V., Cuffaro, H. K., Schultz, S., Silin, J. G., & Wickens, E. (1996). Toward a most thorough understanding of the world: Sexual orientation and early childhood education. *Harvard Educational Review, 66*(2), 271–293.

Casper, V., & Schultz, S. (1999). *Gay parents/straight schools: Building communication and trust.* New York: Teachers College Press.

Clausen, J. (1997). *Beyond gay or straight: Understanding sexual orientation.* Philadelphia: Chelsea House.

Clay, J. (1990). Working with lesbian and gay parents and their children. *Young Children, 45*(2), 31–35.

Corbett, S. (1993). A complicated bias. *Young Children, 48*(3), 29–31.

Derman-Sparks, L. (1989). *Anti-bias curriculum: Tools for empowering young children.* Washington, DC: National Association for the Education of Young Children.

Goodman, J. M. (1993). Lesbian, gay and bisexual issues in education: A personal view. *Thrust for Educational Leadership,* pp. 24–28.

King, J. R. (1997). Keeping it quiet: Gay teachers in the primary grades. In J. Tobin (Ed.), *Making a place for pleasure in early childhood education* (pp. 235–250). New Haven: Yale University Press.

Lewis, M. (1987). Early sex role behavior and school age adjustment. In J. M. Reinisch, L. A. Rosenblum, & S. A. Sanders (Eds.), *Masculinity/femininity: Basic perspectives* (pp. 202–226). New York: Oxford University Press.

Lively, V., & Lively, E. (1991). *Sexual development of young children.* Albany, NY: Delmar.

Lorde, A. (1983). There is no hierarchy of oppressions. *Interracial Books for Children Bulletin, 14*(3 & 4), 9.

Mondimore, F. M. (1996). *A natural history of homosexuality.* Baltimore: Johns Hopkins University Press.

Pogrebin, L. C. (1980). *Growing up free: Raising your child in the eighties.* New York: Bantam Books.

Rubin, G. (1984). Thinking sex: Notes for a radical theory of the politics of sexuality. In C. S. Vance (Ed.), *Pleasure and danger: Exploring female sexuality* (pp. 267–319). Boston: Routledge.

Savin-Williams, R. C. (1995). Lesbian, gay male, and bisexual adolescents. In

A. R. D'Augelli & C. J. Patterson (Eds.), *Lesbian, gay, and bisexual identities over the lifespan: Psychological perspectives* (pp. 165–189). New York: Oxford University Press.

Sears, J. T. (1997). Thinking critically/intervening effectively about heterosexism and homophobia: A twenty-five year research retrospective. In J. T. Sears (Ed.), *Overcoming heterosexism and homophobia: Strategies that work* (pp. 13–48). New York: Columbia University Press.

Sedgwick, E. K. (1990). *Epistemology of the closet.* Berkeley: University of California Press.

Silin, J. G. (1995). *Sex, death, and the education of children: Our passion for ignorance in the age of AIDS.* New York: Teachers College Press.

Strickland, B. R. (1995). Research on sexual orientation and human development: A commentary. *Developmental Psychology, 31*(1), 137–140.

Tierney, W. G. (1997). *Academic outlaws: Queer theory and cultural studies in the academy.* Thousand Oaks, CA: Sage.

Tobin, J. (1997). Playing doctor in two cultures: The United States and Ireland. In J. Tobin (Ed.), *Making a place for pleasure in early childhood education* (pp. 119–158). New Haven: Yale University Press.

Wickens, E. (1993). Penny's question: I will have a child in my class with two moms—What do you know about this? *Young Children, 48*(3), 25–28.

Williams, W. L. (1997). Introduction. In J. T. Sears (Ed.), *Overcoming heterosexism and homophobia: Strategies that work* (pp. 1–10). New York: Columbia University Press.

Wolfe, A. (1998, February 8). The homosexual exception. *New York Times Magazine,* pp. 46–47.

CHAPTER 8

Fractured or Manufactured: Gendered Identities and Culture in the Early Years

Patrick Hughes & Glenda Mac Naughton

GENDER TOUCHES and constructs young children's lives in a myriad of ways. Over 40 years, researchers have established that gender constructs young children's learning; their play styles; their friends and experiences; their expectations, hopes, and desires; and their possibilities. In the majority of instances, these "effects" of gender reinforce traditionally gendered ways of being. This knowledge has resulted in regular advice to classroom teachers about how to construct nontraditionally gendered and anti-sexist identities with young children. Despite nearly 40 years of such advice (Mac Naughton, in press), early childhood classroom teachers and parents remain perplexed about why so many young children still actively seek and construct traditionally gendered ways of being, despite adults' efforts to offer alternatives.

This chapter explores this question through a case study of the gendered effects of Barbie in young children's lives. It suggests that early childhood teachers' work in this area has been guided by flawed models of gendered identity formation. An alternative model of identity formation is offered as a starting point for early childhood teachers who wish to rethink their approaches to the gendering of identity in their classrooms.

BARBIE: SOME FACTS AND FIGURES

Barbie has been and continues to be one of the most successful dolls in the toy industry. Since her release by Mattel in 1959, her success has been evident in her market reach: nine out of ten girls in the United States own at least one Barbie (Chauchard-Stuart, 1996); in Australia Barbie has represented four of the top-ten-selling dolls at Toys R Us (Strolling Fun Barbie—number one; Teacher Barbie—number two; Baywatch Barbie—number five; and Doctor Barbie—number six) (Brown, 1996). More facts and figures highlight Barbie's pervasiveness:

- Barbie products generate $1 billion worth of sales each year (Jones, 1995), and there are currently more than 600 million Barbie dolls in the world (Allen, 1996).
- If the Barbie dolls sold to date worldwide were laid end to end, they would circumnavigate the planet at the equator 50 times (Adams, 1996).
- Every second of every day, two Barbie dolls are sold somewhere in the world (Carafella, 1996). To meet this demand, Mattel manufactures about 60,000 dolls each day (Adams, 1996).

In Australia, there are already more Barbie dolls than there are people. Australians have bought 20 million Barbie dolls (Allen, 1996), with Australian sales accounting for $40 million annually.

This level of success is the result of active marketing strategies and substantial promotional budgets. Each year Mattel releases up to 25 new Barbie dolls and over 1,200 new outfits for Barbie (Brown, 1996). Indeed, in 1996 Mattel increased its promotional budget for dolls by 20%, with $5 million allocated to promoting Barbie in Australia alone (Brown, 1996). Barbie's commercial success is unquestionable, but there has been fierce international debate—we will call it "the Barbie debate"—about Barbie's significance, especially the impact on young children's gendered identity or sense of self. The Barbie debate is an interesting example of how people think about relationships between young children's gendered identities and popular culture. Each side of the debate is based on a particular model of identity formation (a "sponge" model or a "free market" model), with each having significant implications for the role of early childhood educators. In the next section, we outline the debate and the models of identity implied. Following the discussion of more modernist views of identity, we examine how feminist poststructuralism could recast the debate and generate new possibilities for the roles of early childhood teachers.

CHILDREN: SPONGES OR FREE AGENTS?

There is much debate about whether Barbie is a positive or negative influence on children's developing sense of self. Some people (including Mattel) argue that Barbie offers young girls a wide variety of positive occupational role models (Chauchard-Stuart, 1996). For instance, did you know that Barbie was the first female U.S. astronaut? "Astronaut Barbie" took off in 1965. Since then, Barbie has had many nontraditional occupations, including surgeon, Olympic athlete, rock star, UNICEF ambassador, and air force squadron leader (Allen, 1996).

Opponents argue that Barbie presents children with negative, problematic senses of who they are and who they can be. Specifically, they argue that Barbie embodies strong sex-role stereotypes that reinforce ultra-feminine ways of being and an image of woman as sex object (Dixon, 1987). In Barbie's world, you get your man or your job if you can accessorize well, groom well, and look glamorous (Carlsson-Paige & Levin, 1990; Dixon, 1987). Further, Barbie offers a very upper-class view of life: never dressed for the factory floor, only for high-paying, middle-class and upper-class jobs; always living in large, well-appointed houses; and with cars (including a Porsche) and clothes in the luxury bracket. Finally, Ducille (1994) has accused Barbie of inducting children into a consumer culture: "I regard Barbie and similar dolls . . . as objects that do the dirty work of patriarchy and capitalism in the most insidious way—in the guise of children's play" (p. 48).

While each side in this aspect of the Barbie debate fiercely contests the other's arguments, both sides agree that young children form their identity through observing and absorbing social messages from their surroundings. Both sides regard identity formation as an unthinking process in which children uncritically observe and absorb messages about what society wants them to be, from social institutions such as the family, the media, and the toy industry. From this perspective, children are ever-alert sponges who soak up the social environment around them (see, e.g., Derman-Sparks, 1989; Millam, 1996). Thus, Barbie supporters argue that Barbie's range of positive occupations transmits positive messages that girls can do anything and be anyone, and that, fortunately, children "soak up" these positive messages. In contrast, her critics argue that Barbie products transmit problematic—sometimes negative—messages about gender, race, and class, and that, unfortunately, children soak up these problematic messages.

In sponge models, identity formation is a passive process; young children automatically soak up whatever messages they encounter. In some ways, this is a potentially attractive proposition for teachers, because it implies that they can have a very high degree of control over the identities of the children in their classrooms. In sponge models, the messages and experiences that young children encounter are crucial to the development of their identity, so the teacher's role is to arrange the classroom and the curriculum so that children encounter the "right" messages and experiences. From another perspective, that is a minimal, restricted role for a teacher. She or he is reduced almost to the status of a removalist, merely arranging furniture, curriculum materials, and other resources, then standing back while the children soak up their messages. What place has pedagogy when learning is an essentially passive activity?

As if to challenge the passivity of sponge models, another strand of the Barbie debate gives young children an active role in forming their identities. In this strand, debate concerns the extent to which young children are free to form their identities and, therefore, the extent to which Barbie products can influence the formation of their identities. Some people argue that children make up their own minds about things and, by extension, that they can form their own identities. For these people, children actively construct their own ideas of who they can be and should be from their own unique experiences, including their relationships with social institutions such as the family, the media, and the toy industry. In this model, the child is not a mere product of social forces, but is, instead, a free agent, constructing a sense of self from a variety of freely available options. Consequently, we will call this the "free agent in a free market" model of identity formation. This model assumes that children create their own unique identities from their own unique understandings of issues such as gender, race, and class. Understandings are believed to emanate from various sources, including children's peers, their parents, and social institutions. Children are not "taken in" by social institutions or by companies like Mattel. Instead, they become who and what they want to.

Hekman (1991) described the individual implied by this model as a "transcendental constitutor" (p. 48), because she or he appears able to transcend her or his particular social and material circumstances and to constitute her- or himself irrespective of what society says to do or to be. From this perspective, Barbie is harmless and inconsequential, with little long-term effect on children (Carafella, 1996; Lord, 1995). A particular child's identity *may* correspond with particular messages in the environment, but it need not, and there is no guarantee that it will—a child will be who she or he wants to be. Thus, when a child encounters the gender messages that Mattel embodies in Barbie, she or he may incorporate those messages in a sense of self—but she or he may not.

The free-agent model presents the child as an active and creative agent, actively and creatively choosing who and what she or he wants to be, rather than the passive product of social forces implied by the sponge model. This is an unattractive proposition for teachers, because it implies that they can have little, if any, control over the identities of the children in their classrooms. If the child is a free agent, constructing meanings and identity through her or his own inner psychological processes, then the educator has no part to play other than providing the "right" experiences. What place has pedagogy when learning is an essentially individual, inner-directed activity? More generally, however, the free-agent model appears very attractive, not least because it resembles the broader, liberal-humanist ideology of consumer sovereignty, which regards a product's success or failure in free markets as the clearest expression of a society's will and preferences. The individual, "active" young child, freely choosing identities within a theoretical infinity of options, corresponds with the individual consumer, freely choosing commodities within a theoretical infinity of options offered by free markets. However, just as ideals of consumer sovereignty face markets dominated by a handful of major firms, free-agent models of identity formation face mounting evidence that children's race, gender, and class influence their identities.

TIGHTER MARKETS, NARROWER IDENTITIES?

Liberal-humanist notions of consumer sovereignty are being undermined in the cultural and communications industries (as in other industries) by two tendencies, each giving cultural producers greater power to determine the meaning and significance of cultural products, from movies to toys. First, ownership is becoming increasingly concentrated and integrated into oligopolies. For example, half a dozen transnational firms such as News Corporation and CNN dominate the film and television sector. Another handful—including, of course, Mattel and Toys R Us—dominate the production and distribution of toys. The tighter the oligopolies and the more inclusive the alliances, the harder it is for new firms, new products, and new discourses to break in. This structural and discursive integration increases the power of major firms such as Mattel to determine how a particular product is consumed because it increases their ability to channel consumption through the relatively narrow range of discourses circulating as their marketing strategies (Biltereyst, 1995; Deacon & Golding, 1994; Hughes, 1995).

The second tendency undermining consumer sovereignty is that alliances between firms are replacing competition between them (Hughes, 1997; Michalet, 1991; Storper, 1993). Companies form these alliances to share the often-enormous costs of developing new technologies or new products or to cross-market each other's products—using one product to promote one or more other products. Sometimes this cross-marketing happens in-range, that is, between products in the same range; sometimes it happens cross-range, that is, between products in different ranges. Mattel has created several examples of in-range and cross-range, cross-marketing alliances around Barbie. In-range cross-marketing underlies Barbie's "friends" such as Midge (1963) and Skipper (1964) as well as Ken's friend Allan (1963), each of whom in some way "refers" to one or more other characters in the Barbie stable, although the references demand little characterization. Indeed, in a rare critical moment in his hagiography of Barbie (and, implicitly, of Mattel), Billy Boy (1987) remarked that a friend of either Barbie or Ken was defined in terms of their ability to wear each other's clothes—another example of roles reduced to costumes! Not for nothing was Barbie's first CD (launched in 1991) called "The Look" (Rand, 1995)!

Cross-range cross-marketing links Barbie with other popular cultural products made by other manufacturers, for example, "Baywatch Barbie"—complete with characters and ocean-blue backdrop—and "Pizza Hut Barbie." The latter features not just the trademark architecture of the universal Pizza Hut, but also the Pepsi Cola trademark that indicates the alliance between alleged competitors in the fast-food industry. In another twist, Pepsi Cola owns KFC—another competitor of Pizza Hut. And in one more twist, Mattel's 1990 annual report discussed new cross-marketing arrangements with Pepsi Cola's major competitor, Coca Cola, as well as with Mastercard (Rand, 1995). So Barbie's "friends" include not just Ken and Midge but Pamela Anderson (star of "Baywatch") and Pepsi Cola, each of whom helps Mattel to become an increasingly significant source of discourses about the world (including, of course, discourses about itself) and about culture as consumption.

In another cross-range form of cross-marketing, Mattel has produced a series of exclusive, limited-edition Barbies. Some of these
have been linked to specific stores, including J. C. Penney, F. A. O.
Schwarz, Sears, Toys R Us, and Child World/Children's Palace. Others
have been linked to wholesale and/or mail order firms, including the
Wholesale Club and Service Merchandise. Mattel also created a Victo-
rian Elegance Barbie for Hallmark cards. Finally, Mattel also created a
series of Barbies for use as "rewards" for what sometimes is called
consumer loyalty. On the basis of a certain number of product points
or proofs of purchase, Kool-Aid powdered drinks has offered two different Wacky Warehouse Barbies. Little Debbie Snack Cakes has Little
Debbie Barbie, and Kraft cheese has offered Cheese and Macaroni Barbie. In addition, Disneyland, Walt Disney World, and Euro-Disney re-
sorts have had a series of Disney Fun Barbies available only at their
theme parks (Fennick, 1996).

In these circumstances, it is increasingly difficult to assert that
consumers actively make their own meanings of cultural products. Indeed, much consumption relates in some way to marketing strategies
such as packaging, retail presentation, advertising, and cross-marketing, which seek to associate particular products with particular identities. A consumer experiences one or more of these marketing-based
identities directly and/or indirectly from peers, family, and so forth.
However, the degree to which specific consumers recognize and adopt
as their own one or more identities associated with a particular product will depend on their access to particular discourses within which
to understand the product and its associated identities (Roscoe,
Marshall, & Gleeson, 1995). As Hughes (1996) has argued, a cultural
product's commercial success depends on its ability to resonate with
consumers' identities—indeed, to insinuate itself into consumers' continuing (re-)construction of their identities:

> The more that major corporations can dominate or even determine the
> repertoire of discourses within and through which audiences (re-)con-
> struct their subjectivities, and the more that discourses within that reper-
> toire equate subjectivity/ies with specific commodities, the more the cor-
> porations can "produce" particular subjectivities geared to purchasing
> those specific commodities. (pp. 96 –97)

In equivalent changes around identity formation, free-agent models of
identity formation increasingly confront evidence that children's race,
gender, and class influence the messages they are exposed to, the ones
they attend to, and the ones they privilege in public (Mac Naughton,
2000).

Despite the fact that the models of identity formation underlying the Barbie debate are simplistic and offer little role to educators, many mainstream early childhood texts present them uncritically (e.g., Millam, 1996). Indeed, mainstream thinking about gendered identity formation offers educators so little room to significantly influence gendering that it is not surprising that many early childhood teachers resist working for gender equity. When feminist poststructuralists have criticized mainstream models of gendered identity formation, they have redefined "identity" as a political issue and have posed alternative metaphors through which to explain relationships between the individual and social institutions (Alloway, 1995; Davies, 1989; Gherardi, 1996; Hekman, 1991).

RETHINKING GENDERED IDENTITY FORMATION
THROUGH FEMINIST POSTSTRUCTURALISM

Since the late 1980s, feminist poststructuralists have criticized sponge models of identity formation for their simplistic view of relationships between individuals' understandings of themselves and their social and cultural contexts (e.g., Davies, 1989, 1993; Lloyd & Duveen, 1992). They have argued that sponge models present children as merely "a product of social forces" (Hekman, 1991, p. 45), with little or no ability to do other than to think and feel what they are told by society. Put simply, the sponge model implies that individuals become what society wants them to be. However, children receive many different and often-conflicting messages from many different sources about who and how to be. For instance, children may receive very different messages from family, peers, and other institutions such as the early childhood center or the media about what is "normal" in terms of gender, race, and ability. In these circumstances, how can we account for the "differentiated gender [and other] identities" (Lloyd & Duveen, 1992, p. 183) that children demonstrate? If young children simply soak up these messages, how do they cope when they receive differing and contradictory expectations and messages? For example, when girls play with Barbie products, how do they cope when some messages tell them that being female is a matter of appearance, while other messages tell them that girls can be anyone and do anything they wish?

In her pioneering work on identity construction in early childhood, Davies (1989, 1993) argued that sponge explanations of relationships between the individual and the social are inadequate because they cannot answer four general questions about how children understand the world. For illustration, we have translated each of Davies's general questions into a specific example concerning Barbie:

- How does the child handle contradictory understandings (e.g., "Barbie is good for you" and "Barbie is bad for you")?
- How does the child choose between dominant and alternative understandings (e.g., related to gender and Barbie products)?
- How does the child resist or reject dominant understandings (e.g., of gender constructed by Mattel in and through Barbie)?
- What influences the child to reject dominant or alternative understandings (e.g., of Barbie products)?

Identity as Multiple, Contradictory, and Dynamic

Feminist poststructuralist theorists such as Davies (1993) have redefined identity. They have challenged the notion that we have a single, coherent, fixed identity that, once acquired, stays with us for life, arguing instead that

- Identity is multiple ("identities"). It has many facets, including gender, race, ethnicity, class, sexuality, ability, geographical location, and so on.
- Identity is (at least potentially) contradictory. Its many facets are not necessarily coherent and often can conflict with each other.
- Identity is dynamic. It is never complete and fixed, but is always changing and in the process of being formed.

If identity is multiple, contradictory, and dynamic, then children are likely to create multiple, contradictory, and changeable identities through their play—including their play with Barbie. From a feminist poststructuralist viewpoint, then, play with Barbie is neither inherently good nor inherently bad. Instead, children are likely to experience such play and understand it in shifting and contradictory ways.

In redefining identity as multiple, contradictory, and dynamic, feminist poststructuralists have politicized identity formation. They have argued that identity is constituted in and by social relations of gender, sexuality, class, and race, and that each of us lives our gendered, sexualized, "classed," and "raced" identities in and through the power relations that constitute our daily lives. Their beginning point is that individuals are inseparable from social institutions; they do not simply interact but are interdependent and mutually constituting. In-

dividuals are born into already-existing social worlds consisting of social structures, social processes, and social meanings. The individual
does not and cannot exist outside of the social, nor can the social exist
over and above the individual.

Further, feminist poststructuralists have emphasized that identity
formation is not just an abstract, cognitive exercise but is inherently
emotional. Davies (1993) emphasized the role of desire in creating identities and the importance of the pleasures associated with different identities. She argued that developing identities involves learning to

> read and interpret the landscape of the social world, and to embody, to
> live, to experience, to know, to desire as one's own, to take pleasure in
> the world, as it is made knowable through the available discourses, social
> structures and practices. (p. 17)

In other words, as children construct their identities, they encounter
various meanings and must actively do the following:

- Read, interpret, and understand those meanings
- Desire or reject them
- Live, embody, and express the meanings they desire by taking
  them up as their own
- By doing so, gain pleasure from them

This is not to say that children are free to construct any meanings
or any identities they wish. The meanings and identities that children
can construct may be many and variable, *but* they are restricted to the
alternatives to which the children have access. This is more than just
a truism. Children do not enter a free market of ideas but a market in
which some meanings are more available, more desirable, more recog-
nizable, more pleasurable, and therefore more powerful than others.
Further, as we've just seen, the market of ideas is characterized by
differential access—gender, sexuality, class, and "race" influence the
ideas one encounters and finds attractive. Therefore, while feminist
poststructuralists pose the child as an active agent forming her or his
own identity, they emphasize that such agency is experienced and exercised within and through definite social categories such as gender,
race, and class, thereby avoiding the trap of a naive humanism.

Feminist poststructuralism could be used inappropriately to respond to the perceived inadequacies of the sponge and free-agent models. Its emphasis on the role of social categories could be translated
into a simplistic argument that each individual child's identity con-

sists of a specific combination of gender, race, and class. Rather than rethinking identity formation, this would merely introduce new variables of gender, race, and class into the existing individualistic model of identity that dominates early childhood education. Alternatively, the emphasis of feminist poststructuralism on the role of social categories could be translated into an argument that children's identity is influenced or even determined by their gender, race, and class. This would reduce those social categories—always contingent on and contributing to specific social and material circumstances—to essential human characteristics and would reduce identity to a particular combination of those social categories in a particular individual. To avoid such reductionism, we need to theorize just how those social categories are individually and collectively involved in the continuing process of identity formation in children and adults. More specifically, we need to ask:

- How have particular discourses of gender, of race, of class, and so forth, achieved their current influence (or lack thereof)?
- How have particular discourses of gender, of race, of class, and so forth, come to be accessible to specific individuals at a particular site?
- How are particular discourses of gender, of race, of class, and so forth, involved in the construction of an individual's identity(ies) at a particular site?
- How, in turn, does the construction of an individual's identity at a particular site reinforce and/or challenge the influence of each discourse?

This theorizing is a daunting task and certainly beyond the scope of this chapter. However, we can begin to approach it by exploring the formation and circulation of what we will call the "social repertoire of discourses," illustrating our argument with reference to Barbie products.

Social Repertoire of Discourses

The social repertoire of discourses is the sum total of discourses present in one form or another within which a social category such as gender is conceptualized at a particular sociohistorical moment. An individual assembles her or his own specific discursive repertoire by adopting as her or his own one or more of those discourses circulating within the social repertoire. This is not to say that identity formation occurs in the equivalent of a free market of ideas. Instead, the individual encounters a social repertoire of discourses in which certain discourses are more familiar, more accessible, more influential, and therefore more attractive than others because they have a stronger institutional base. The cultural and communications industries form an institutional base for the production and circulation of discourses that is increasing in importance as the ownership and control of these industries becomes more concentrated and integrated. Consequently, a focus on the *accessibility* and *influence* of particular discourses almost inevitably leads to an examination of the structure and operation of those industries.

For decades, the ownership and control of the cultural and communications industries—like those of many other industries—have become increasingly concentrated and integrated. This has enabled a decreasing number of major corporations—including Mattel, as well as Disney, Sony, Time–Warner, and News Corporation—to increasingly influence the formation and circulation of the social repertoire of discourses through cultural products, including newspapers, radio and television program, films, books, CDs, videos, and computer games. Barbie offers several instances of that general tendency for producers to discursively dominate consumption. At an obvious level, Mattel's influence on the toy industry and, thus, on the range of consumption choices is illustrated by the rash of Barbie clones created by other firms. Examples include Hasbro's "Sindy" and DIC's "Sailor Moon," a doll promoted via an eponymous cartoon that, in Australia in July 1996, was the highest-rating cartoon on Channel 7's children's program "Agro's Cartoon Connection." At a less obvious level, Mattel discursively dominates consumption by its insistence on the child's ability to "make" Barbie what she wants. Fennick (1996) has reported the remark of Ruth Handler (joint creator of Barbie) that she wanted each child to create "her own" personalities for Barbie, using products with the Barbie brand name:

> Mrs. Handler wanted the child to develop her own perception of what Barbie should be like on [sic] her dolls. Therefore, Barbie doll's clothing and accessories were created with a wide variety of possibilities in mind. For example, she could be a career girl, a teenage model, a torch singer or a college co-ed. The endless choices were left up to the doll's owner. . . . Ruth Handler's plan for her dream doll also included a chic up-to-date wardrobe of the best possible quality. . . . The first series of Barbie clothing designs . . . were taken directly from the Paris showrooms of the late 1950s and early 1960s. Dior, Chanel, Balenciaga, Chiaparelli and

other couturiers served as inspiration for Mattel's design team. (pp. 14, 16)

Thus, a child could "make" early Barbies into anything she wished by choosing among Barbie's accessories. At that time, however, those accessories just happened to consist of copies of haute couture fashion, encouraging consumption to take the form of emulation of particular classes and shapes of women. Barbie's links with the fashion industry have been noted in both celebratory and analytical ways (e.g., Billy Boy, 1987; Craik, 1988/89, respectively), and dressing and undressing Barbie have always been at least a feature of play with her and sometimes its exclusive focus. No surprise, then, that Mattel backs its claims that Barbie can "be" a diversity of roles with the evidence of her diverse wardrobe. For example:

- In 1985, Mattel launched Day-to-Night Barbie with the slogan, "We Girls Can Do Anything," and with a range of costumes for an executive, a dress designer, a TV news reporter, a vet, and a teacher.
- In 1990, Mattel launched Flight Time Barbie ("who doubles as a pilot and flight attendant—with a sparkly after-hours outfit").
- In 1991, Lights 'n' Lace Barbie appeared, suitably dressed as a music video star. Also in 1991, "We Girls Can Do Anything" reappeared as a board game in which, however, "anything" was restricted to "a glamorous actress, a graceful ballerina, an out-of-this-world pilot," or a doctor, musician, or fashion designer (Mitchell & Reid-Walsh, 1995).

Any doubt as to the discursive force of Mattel's slogan is dispelled by considering what *is not said.* "Girls can do anything" just by subscribing to "the American dream" and working hard. No social and economic changes are required—Whites, men, and capitalism can each stay as they are. However, Barbie rarely has to strive for anything. Each of her careers comes ready-made with its characteristic costume, and indeed Barbie seems to predate Madonna in reducing roles to costumes. Noting that Mattel sells more Barbie wedding dresses than any other costume (5 million by 1991), Rand (1995) observed that Mattel does not "force" Barbie to marry. Instead, "it clothes her in garments and ideology that make marriage seem like her natural, her most desirable, and her freely-chosen destiny—the destiny that Barbie fantasizes about" (p. 90). Rand shrewdly summarized the ability of the costumes to influence—perhaps predetermine—consumers' relationships with this product and its allegedly infinite meanings as follows: "Barbie can be anything but wouldn't it be especially fun to make her a rock star with this Lights 'n' Lace outfit and stage that you can buy?" (p. 9).

TOWARD A NEW MODEL OF IDENTITY FORMATION: NEW ROLES FOR TEACHERS?

Our analysis of the production and consumption of Barbie shows that when we theorize identity, we need to acknowledge young children's active creation of their identities as well as the structural, material constraints on that activity. Thus, any new model of identity formation must theorize it as a variable outcome of a balance between two forces:

- Children's active creation of identities within the discourses that they have acquired as a result of their specific social and material circumstances.
- The increasing ability of major corporations to influence the availability of particular discourses of identity within which to make sense of their products.

With these forces in mind, we can formulate an alternative, general model of identity formation thus:

Individuals actively and continuously construct and reconstruct their identity(ies) or sense(s) of self, but they do so within discursive repertoires that are increasingly liable to be dominated by the major corporations within the cultural and communications industries.

This alternative model of identity formation attempts to integrate the following three phenomena from our notion of constrained consumer sovereignty:

- The politicization of identity
- The intersections between cultural consumption and the formation of politicized identities
- The intersections between consumers' active meaning production and the social and material conditions in which it is exercised (Hughes & Mac Naughton, 2000)

These three phenomena have clear pedagogic implications for teachers who are rethinking their role in young children's gendered identity formation. Teachers can go beyond role modeling or the presentation of alternative gender images and messages to young children. Teachers can actively engage with young children in the examination and negotiation of gendered cultural meanings, so that teachers' understandings of gender identity become part of the experiences of the children in their classrooms.

We will conclude with several possible starting points for teachers in this work. Each point invites teachers of young children to actively seek, negotiate, and debate cultural and political meanings tied to gender. Teachers can begin by engaging in the following activities:

- Observe how young children's gender identity is politicized through the cultural products, texts, and experiences they consume during their daily life in the classroom. Use this observation to initiate conversations with children about how they make sense of those cultural products, texts, and experiences.
- Introduce cultural products, texts, and experiences that increase the diversity of gender politics that children can consume. Share with children different ways to understand culturally gendered issues and messages.
- Debate with children the pros and cons of different ways of being gendered.

One way to explore this model of identity formation would be to invite Barbie into the classroom in order to use her and children's lived experiences. Indeed, teachers can begin their active engagement in gendered meaning construction with young children by using a variety of cultural products, from Pocahontas to Pokemon. We hope this model helps teachers to re-imagine their role in young children's identity formation and to enable a diversity of gendered identities to flourish in their classrooms.

REFERENCES

Adams, P. (1996, November 11). Barb-aryan hordes. *The Weekend Australian*, pp. 2–3.
Allen, F. (1996, July 11). What a doll. *Herald Sun*, pp. 70–71.
Alloway, N. (1995). *Foundation stones: The construction of gender in early childhood.* Carleton, Victoria: Curriculum Corporation.
Billy Boy (1987). *Barbie: Her life and times.* New York: Gown Books.
Biltereyst, D. (1995). Qualitative audience research and transnational media

effects: A new paradigm? *European Journal of Communication, 10*(2), 245–270.

Brown, S. (1996). Babes in toyland. *The Sunday Age*, p. 6.

Carafella, J. (1996, May 15). Why Barbie is a nerd. *The Age*, p. 23.

Carlsson-Paige, N., & Levin, N. (1990). *Who's calling the shots? How to respond effectively to children's fascination with war plays and war toys.* Gabriola Island, British Columbia: New Society.

Chauchard-Stuart, S. (1996, December 23). Barbie goes hi-tech. *The Independent Tabloid*, p. 8.

Craik, J. (1988/89, December). Barbie at the barricades. *Australian Left Review*, pp. 16–18.

Davies, B. (1989). *Frogs and snails and feminist tales: Preschool children and gender.* North Sydney, NSW: Allen & Unwin.

Davies, B. (1993). *Shards of glass: Children reading and writing beyond gendered identities.* North Sydney, NSW: Allen & Unwin.

Deacon, D., & Golding, P. (1994). *Taxation and representation: Political communication, the media and the poll tax.* London: John Libbey.

Derman-Sparks, L. (1989). *The anti-bias curriculum: Tools for empowering young children.* Washington, DC: National Association for the Education of Young Children.

Dixon, B. (1987, December 15). Fashion for the formula female. *The Morning Star*, p. 5.

Ducille, A. (1994). Dyes and dolls. *Difference, 6*(1), 46–48.

Fennick, J. (1996). *The collectible Barbie doll.* London: New Burlington Books.

Gherardi, S. (1996). Gendered organizational cultures: Narratives of women travelors in a male world. *Gender, Work and Organisation, 3*(4), 187–201.

Hekman, S. (1991). Reconstituting the subject: Feminism, modernism, and postmodernism. *Hypatia, 6*(2), 44–63.

Hughes, P. (1995, July 5–7). *Reinforcing "core" discursive repertoires: Evaluating press representations of child care accreditation policy.* Paper presented at Australian and New Zealand Communication Association Conference, Perth.

Hughes, P. (1996). Producing audiences: Towards a political economy of subjectivities. *Media International Australia, 80*, 93–98.

Hughes, P. (1997). Can governments weather the storm in the new communications climate? *Australian Journal of Public Administration, 56*(4), 78–86.

Hughes, P., & Mac Naughton, G. (2000). Identity-formation and popular culture: Learning lessons from Barbie. *Journal of Curriculum Theorizing, 16*(3), 57–68.

Jones, M. (1995, March 23). Pristine Barbie image revised for '90s buyer. *The Age*, p. 26.

Lloyd, B., & Duveen, G. (1992). *Gender identities and education: The impact of starting school.* Hertfordshire: Harvester Wheatsheaf.

Lord, M. (1995). *Forever Barbie: The unauthorized biography of a real doll.* New York: Avon.

Mac Naughton, G. (2000, January 29–30). *"Blushes and birthday parties": Telling silences in young children's constructions of "race."* Paper presented to the Australian Research in Early Childhood Education Annual Conference, Canberra.

Mac Naughton, G. (in press). Silences, sex-roles and subjectivities: 40 years of gender in the Australian Journal of Early Childhood. *Australian Journal of Early Childhood.*

Michalet, C. A. (1991). Strategic partnerships and the changing internationalization process. In L. Mytela (Ed.), *Strategic partnership: States, firms and international competition* (pp. 35–50). Madison & Teaneck, NJ: Farleigh Dickinson University Press.

Millam, R. (1996). *Anti-discriminatory practice: A guide for workers in childcare and education.* London: Cassell Books.

Mitchell, C., & Reid-Walsh, J. (1995). And I want to thank you Barbie: Barbie as a site for cultural interrogation. *The Review of Education/Pedagogy/ Cultural Studies, 17*(2), 143–155.

Rand, E. (1995). *Barbie's queer accessories.* Raleigh, NC, & London: Duke University Press.

Roscoe, J., Marshall, H., & Gleeson, K. (1995). The television audience: A reconsideration of the taken-for-granted terms, "active," "social" and "critical." *European Journal of Communication, 10*(1), 87–108.

Storper, M. (1993). [Review of *Strategic partnerships: States, firms and international competition*]. *Transnational Corporations, 2*(1), 171–174.

PART IV

Challenging Colonized Identities

CHAPTER 9

Reflections on Collectivism in Early Childhood Teaching in Aotearoa/New Zealand

Jenny Ritchie

LATELY I HAVE been reflecting on the cultural implications of the erosion of a sense of collectivism as a social ethic in
Western society. In *Pigs in Heaven*, Barbara Kingsolver (1993) contrasts a Cherokee woman's social ethic with that of the dominant culture:

> Says Jax, a white male, to Annawake, a Cherokee woman: "So that's your
> guiding myth. Do right by your people or you'll be a pig in heaven."
> Annawake thinks this over. "Yes. I had a hundred and one childhood
> myths and they all added up more or less to 'Do right by your people.' Is
> that so bad?" Jax replies: "Myths are myths. They're good if they work for
> you, and bad if they don't." Asks Annawake: "What are yours?" and Jax
> replies, "Oh, you know, I heard the usual American thing. If you're indus-
> trious and have clean thoughts you will grow up to be vice president of
> Motorola," which Annawake sums up as, "Do right by yourself." (p. 88)

NEW RIGHT INDIVIDUALISM

New Right government ideology has resulted in some very obvious
restructuring of educational institutions in my country, but I also won-

der how, in more insidious ways, this may be influencing our work
with young children in early childhood education. Recently, in a local-
ity of New Zealand, the regional management organization imposed a
policy that changed a long-standing practice in the local public kindergartens of having, at a midpoint within the session, a shared "fruit
time." Children would be encouraged to gather together, choose a
piece of fruit, and sit on a mat to eat while a teacher read them a story.
The new policy is that instead of each child contributing a piece of
fruit to be shared, each child brings his or her own individual snack.
Children may choose when they wish to obtain their snack, and go to
the set eating area. They may sit alone or join a small group of peers.
A teacher may or may not join them. Some kindergartens resisted this
new policy. Teachers and parents liked the sense of community and
sharing that the previous arrangement had provided. A shared time for
eating is also consistent with *tikanga Māori* (Māori values and cultural
practices, the customs that are "right," *tika*, for Māori), and the New
Zealand early childhood curriculum strand of "belonging" (Ministry
of Education, 1996). However, these teachers' challenges to the new
policy were overruled by management.

I wondered if this was an example of a subtle form of New Right
individualism that was being instituted under the pedagogic guise of
"free choice." Giroux (1995) has described the impact of the New Right
as redefining education "through a corporate ideology that stresses the
primacy of choice over community, competition over cooperation, and
excellence over equity" (p. ix). My understanding of the strength of
collectivism expressed in *tikanga Māori* and my involvement for a
number of years within Māori *whānau* (extended families) and the *Kōhanga Reo* (Māori early childhood language) movement (Tangaere,
1997) have contributed to my discomfort with rampantly individualistic modes of operating. Furthermore, this New Right thrust seems to
me to be yet another manifestation of colonization, imposing such a
blatantly contradictory social ethic onto an indigenous people for
whom collectivity is fundamental to well-being.

My thinking was both supported and challenged when I was privileged to attend the 1998 meeting of the American Educational Research Association in San Diego. In presentations at this conference,
Howard Gardner (1998) advocated a need for socially responsible and
humane creativity as a goal for educators. Peter McLaren and Zeuss
Leonardo (1998) contrasted the individualistic acquisitive orientation
of labor-exploitative capitalism with the "gift-giving" focus of Polynesian societies whose unit of organization is very much the collective

social grouping. Michael Apple (1998) talked about how the possessive individualism of the New Right contributes not only to the loss of collectivity, but to an amnesia regarding the ongoing effects of colonization as they affect social dynamics today. He reminded us that today's struggles are given meaning by the memory of those who died due to colonization.

Humans are social beings, and our very survival as a species is testimony to our collective strength. In promoting a holistic, critical, and constructive postmodernism in education, Shea (1996) suggests that postmodern teachers are intuitively aware of the web of relationships that surround the children with whom they work. This enables them to foster children's agency in terms of understanding and enhancing these relationships. I believe in this intuitive responsiveness, but I see this intuition as a reference point for a proactive social ethic of care and community.

Early childhood teachers and teacher educators in my country are facing an increasingly callous ideology that seeks to remove government from sharing responsibility for nurturing young children and families. The survival strategy that I am proposing is that we develop a counterpervasiveness of collectivity as an overarching guiding principle in our work in teacher education and with young children. Through embracing this proactive stance it may be possible to reactivate the sense of shared social responsibility and social contract that is the foundation of many indigenous societies, and has long been advocated within progressive education by writers such as Dewey (1966). Fay (1987) has suggested an "ecological ideal" of

> a way of living in which people are deeply impressed with the interrelatedness of all things to each other, and have the care and sensitivity which must be taken in dealing with any one member of a system because of the reverberations of any part on all the other parts. (p. 195)

CARE/EDUCATION AS COLLECTIVE ENDEAVOR

The early childhood teaching profession reflects an ethic of caring and service to community. In their daily work, early childhood teachers model, at least subconsciously, values of care and responsibility. However, despite their concern for the well-being of those individual children within their care, my perception is that few early childhood educators consciously attempt to construct a programmatic discourse for providing students with the knowledge, skills, and values they will need, not only to find their own voices but to understand these voices and to use them to constitute themselves as collective social agents. (Giroux & McLaren, 1992, p. 10)

Reflecting on many years of observations and experiences within early childhood centers in Aotearoa/New Zealand (the name Aotearoa is used to reflect the status of Māori as *tāngata whenua*, people of the land), I can recall few examples of teachers involving children in decisions about their daily lives in the ways that Greenberg (1992a, 1992b) and Gerber (1979) have advocated. Without this awareness early childhood teachers are missing opportunities to use the dialogic methods advocated by critical pedagogues more often for older children and adults, because early childhood teachers are coming from a maternalistic orientation that, despite their good intentions, cannot avoid being disempowering to the young children in their care.

Leavitt and Power (1997) relate a litany of graphic and disturbing examples of interactions in day-care centers in the United States. The authors do not discuss the levels of the qualifications held by the teachers and caregivers they studied. I wonder how many were unqualified or poorly qualified staff who had not had opportunities to develop a reflective stance that would enable them to critique their teaching philosophy and interactions. The manipulative and emotionally abusive practices characterized by this uncritiqued "mother knows best" practice are examples of what Jones and Reynolds (1992) have described as a "power on moralizing" approach (p. 50).

The practices that Leavitt and Power (1997) described were disturbing from both individual and social perspectives. I was concerned by the deep disrespect shown to individual children. The child's right to determine even such a fundamental need as going to the bathroom, for example, was being undermined by the focus on controlling children's bodies in line with daily routines, the "temporal order of the day care center," as determined by staff (p. 46). The disapproval exhibited toward the noncompliant child is potentially damaging to integrity and self-esteem. I related this to the Māori concept of *mana*, which is a form of esteem and prestige that is not an individual construct, but is gained, bestowed, or diminished in relation to one's contribution to the group. In many of the incidents described by Leavitt and Power, the teachers maintain control by pitting the children against each other, as in this example: "Look at the way Lily is sitting. I like the way she is sitting. Look how nicely Jared is sitting" (p. 51).

Educators who believe strongly in a child-centered philosophy may find it hard to implement a cooperatively oriented curriculum, for several reasons. Some teachers do not wish to "interfere" with the child's agenda, since they see their responsibility as primarily creating the conditions for learning. They consider their role to be one of setting up a stimulating learning environment and then observing while the children explore in whatever ways they choose, intervening only if the children's behavior is dangerous or otherwise inappropriate. Alternatively, teachers may lack not only the knowledge and commitment, but also the skills to foster cooperation and a collective sense of community within the early childhood program. Greenberg (1992b) has pointed out that a child-centered orientation can become no more than an excuse for a laissez-faire approach. In the New Zealand context, the prevalence of this approach is compounded by the low levels of staff qualifications and resources within the early childhood sector (May & Carr, 1997).

The growing awareness of Vygotskian-derived theory has resulted in more emphasis being placed on the adult's role in facilitating growth within the child's zone of proximal development. The adult role is understood to be one of supporting the child's agenda in a more contingently responsive manner of co-construction of meaning. The responsibility of the educator within the teaching relationship is to articulate goals and to be aware of the opportunities to seize the "inductive moment" (Freire & Shor, 1987, p. 157). I believe that teachers' goals in terms of the facilitation of children's play should include a focus not just on scaffolding the individual child's problem solving, but on fostering children's social skills and collective endeavor.

Values are transmitted to children whether overtly or through the hidden curriculum (McLaren, 1989). Programs such as the anti-bias curriculum (Derman-Sparks, 1989) encourage teachers to be proactive in creating activities that foster a positive orientation toward difference. Noddings (1992) proposes a philosophical framework for the education of children that is focused around "domains of caring." This framework includes caring for self, the environment, nonhuman creatures, and other people; interpersonal skills for assuming responsibilities within groups; and an appreciation of the impact of their own lives on others. These ideas are consistent with my argument that early childhood teachers should take a proactive stance in instigating learning opportunities that will enhance children's sense of collective responsibility.

Gardner (1984) has alerted us to the dynamics of inter- and intrapersonal intelligences, and the interplay between them: "Knowledge of one's place among others can come only from the external community; the child is inextricably impelled to focus on others, as a clue to himself" (p. 248). He believes that intrapersonal skills are important qualities for social facilitators such as parents, teachers, and leaders. He also acknowledges that these are culturally influenced. The implication of this for early childhood teachers is that they must be alerted to the distinctiveness of the cultural world views of the children and families with whom they work, in order to assist children to develop their "capacity to know oneself and to know others" (p. 243).

Research has indicated increased cognitive benefits from the establishment of intersubjectivity and collective thinking arising from children's involvement in collaborative processes (Liu & Greathouse, 1992; Rogoff, 1991). A further advantage of encouraging collective interactions within early childhood programs is that children experience opportunities to work with those who are different from themselves. This may increase their ability to respect and value diversity (Hill, 1994; Liu & Greathouse, 1992), both of which are reasons for a proactive teacher stance and inclusion of this philosophy in teacher education.

THE AOTEAROA/NEW ZEALAND SITUATION

For over 10 years, successive governments in New Zealand have been driven by a particularly fundamentalist version of New Right ideology, characterized by an unquestioned faith in the ability of the free market to control even aspects of provision previously seen as part of a social contract of the welfare state. Hospitals have been run as profit-oriented businesses, with publicly owned television required to return a dividend to the government. Successive policy changes have eroded the ability of early childhood centers to deliver quality programs. Government policy has favored private providers not only of early childhood care and education, but also of teacher education.

A blatant example of the way in which New Right individualism is reaching far beyond the realm of the economic arena, into the very ethos of education, is seen in the inclusion of "competitive skills" as an "essential skill" in the Curriculum Framework for Learning and Assessment in New Zealand Schools (Ministry of Education, 1993). I question the inclusion of competitive skills alongside the other skills deemed "essential," such as communication, numeracy, problem solving, self-management, and so on.

During the same period of government, the Minister of Education introduced a new early childhood service, Parents as First Teachers

(PAFT) (Pihama, 1993). This program offers support to mothers of new infants and young children in their homes. Unlike the existing New Zealand early childhood education services, PAFT had not been a community initiative. PAFT was instead ideologically based in deficit-model programs from the United States, such as Head Start and the Missouri Project. The service was established by the Ministry of Education and initially was delivered by child health nurses, without consultation with the early childhood community within New Zealand. "Poor parenting" was identified as the target of limited government spending. Dealing directly with the families in their homes was considered more cost-efficient than using early childhood center-based services. The individualistic nature of PAFT is a divergence from the collective ethos of early childhood centers, where parents are able to meet together and share experiences, staff work collaboratively in teams, and children mingle with their peers. Furthermore, PAFT has been criticized by Māori educators for being a perpetuation of colonialist assimilation, blatantly overriding Māori aspirations for self-determination as expressed by the *Kōhanga Reo* movement (Pihama, 1993). PAFT also has been seen as an attempt to discourage women from participation in the work force, since funding for PAFT is not allocated to the provision of center-based child care.

Recent approaches to early childhood pedagogy have seen a shift from a reliance on the individualistic cognitive developmentalist theory of Piaget, wherein the child is portrayed as an explorer of the environment, constructing knowledge about the world, to an emphasis on sociocultural contexts as theorized by Vygotsky and others (Rogoff, 1000; Smith, 1993). We must acknowledge, however, that the play-based approaches adopted by early childhood programs in Aotearoa/New Zealand remain strongly influenced by Piagetian constructivism and have tended to focus on fostering independence and autonomy, rather than on interdependence and collaborative skills. Although it may be an oversimplification of Piaget's writings to view them as supporting an "ideology of individualism" (Youniss, 1994, p. 123), this is unfortunately how interpretations of his work have affected the world of early childhood education. Similarly, we have to contend with a Piagetian-derived legacy of "developmentally appropriate" tags that can be very limiting. I have been asked by a thoughtful student whether there is any point in encouraging a 2-year-old "preoperational" child to share, since her interpretation of Piagetian theory led her to believe that the egocentrism of this stage renders children developmentally incapable of this until "concrete operations" begin at around age 7.

TE WHĀRIKI: EARLY CHILDHOOD CURRICULUM

Since August 1998, early childhood services in New Zealand have been required to ensure that their programs are consistent with *Te Whāriki*, the new early childhood curriculum (Ministry of Education, 1996). It is perhaps ironic, and a tribute to the lobbying strength of the early childhood community, that during a decade in which the government has been driven by New Right ideology, a document that is in many ways philosophically opposed to this ideology has been promulgated by that very same government. *Te Whāriki* takes a holistic, integrated approach to early childhood care and education. It was developed from within the early childhood community, with extensive consultation, and in partnership with the Kōhanga Reo National Trust (Carr & May, 1993). According to the project co-directors, Carr and May, "Consideration of social and cultural context was a major source for the model chosen" for *Te Whāriki* (p. 14). The curriculum applies across the diverse range of services within the early childhood sector in New Zealand, including Māori immersion and Pacific Island programs, and applies to children aged 0–5. It has at its core, the principles of empowerment, holistic development, family and community, and relationships. These principles reflect a sense of collectivism, particularly in the emphasis on involving *whānau* (families) and relationships. Interwoven with these principles are the key strands of well-being, belonging, contribution, communication, and exploration.

A strong focus on enhancing relationships between children and others emerges from a reading of the document's goals and learning outcomes. Contribution Goal 3, for example, "Children experience an environment where they are encouraged to learn with and alongside others," contains the following "learning outcomes" for children in early childhood program:

- strategies and skills for initiating, maintaining, and enjoying a relationship with other children—including taking turns, problem-solving, negotiating, taking another's point of view, supporting others, and understanding other people's attitudes and feelings—in a variety of contexts; . . .
- an increasing ability to take another's point of view and to empathise with others;
- a sense of responsibility and respect for the needs and well-being of the group, including taking responsibility for decisions
- an appreciation of the ways in which they can make contributions to groups and to group well-being (Ministry of Education, 1996, p. 70)

This is a less individualistic approach than may be apparent in other early childhood education curricula, such as the traditional Montessori focus on individualized interaction with didactic materials (Lindauer, 1987). Polokow (1992), from her observations within a Montessori program, relates how children were encouraged to perceive their work as separate from others' work with instructions such as: "This is Marissa's work. Marissa, you need to tell Molly, 'No this is my work'" (p. 83). In this scenario, the adult's agenda of prioritizing individualistic ownership interferes with opportunities to facilitate children's preparedness to share (Broadhead, 1997).

The emphasis within *Te Whāriki* on group endeavor can be seen to move beyond constructivist approaches in which the child is viewed as the Piagetian individual explorer/scientist acting on the world. There is an expectation that adults play an active role in supporting young children to acquire an awareness of others, by helping children "to understand other people's attitudes and feelings" (Ministry of Education, 1996, p. 71). Teachers are also to focus on enhancing young children's social skills, by ensuring that the "program encourages cooperative play by providing activities that are more fun and work better when done cooperatively" (Ministry of Education, 1996, p. 71).

Te Whāriki contains a parallel curriculum in Māori that is designed to support Māori immersion programs. Aside from this, there is a commitment, stated in the introduction to the document, that "in early childhood settings, all children should be given the opportunity to develop knowledge and an understanding of the cultural heritages of both partners to Te Tiriti o Waitangi" (p. 9). This bicultural paradigm derives from the Treaty of Waitangi, a document signed in 1840 that led to British colonization of the country, and the subsequent immigration of people from many other countries, who form the "Crown" side of the partnership with the indigenous Māori as treaty "partners."

This strong bicultural focus of the document provides challenges to Western-centric pedagogy. Early childhood teachers are required, for example, to ensure that the program they implement includes "a recognition of Māori ways of knowing and making sense of the world and of respecting and appreciating the natural environment" (Ministry of Education, 1996, p. 82). Most early childhood teachers in New Zealand are *Pākehā* (people with European ancestry) and have little fluency with either the Māori language or Māori cultural traditions. They may lack the knowledge and skills to deliver authenticity in terms of Māori content within the early childhood program. Furthermore, there are questions as to the extent to which a *Päkehä* teacher should presume to offer "expertise" in a Mäori domain.

According to the Mäori anthropologist Peter Buck (1958), traditional Mäori pedagogy was a process of intergenerational transmission. "The elements of a classical education in family and tribal history, mythology, and folklore were thus imparted by male and female *tipuna* [elders] at an early age" (p. 358). This is one of the underlying principles of the *Köhanga Reo* movement, which recognizes that "the key personnel in the *whänau* are the *kaumätua*, the elders, who are 'the mentors, the soothsayers, the peacemakers, the wise ones based on years of experience'" (Tangaere, 1997, p. 42). *Te Whäriki* contains an implicit recognition of the collective nature of Mäori social organization when it states that "adults working with children should demonstrate an understanding of the different *iwi* [tribes] and the meaning of *whänau* [families] and *whanaungatanga* [extended family relationships]" (Ministry of Education, 1996, p. 42). There is also an expectation of empowerment of Mäori families through involvement in the early childhood center program and decision making. It is possible that *Päkehä* teachers, by creating a climate that invites the involvement of Mäori extended families, may enable the processes described by Peter Buck to be facilitated within mainstream early childhood settings, as occurs within *Köhanga Reo*.

FACILITATING COLLECTIVISM IN EARLY CHILDHOOD

In my work within our early childhood teacher education program, I encourage students to critique the ideology of rugged individualism that tends to be a characteristic of *Päkehä* heritage, and the individualistic orientation of much of the current child-centered early childhood pedagogy. Students appear to find it easy to recall occasions from their own childhood experiences when they were encouraged to demonstrate independence and autonomy, but much harder to furnish examples of instances when they were encouraged to interact cooperatively. Similarly, when they write an essay on the subject of facilitating cooperative play, they tend to focus on individual rather than social benefits of cooperative play.

We explore ways that teachers' planning of the environment and arrangements for play opportunities can foster children's collective endeavor. Katz and McClellan (1991) point out the role of structural factors such as group size, arrangement of space, provision of equipment, ratios of adults to children, and age ranges. For example, the simple matter of the arrangement of the play-dough table for the children's use can enhance or inhibit cooperative exchanges. Often the teacher has carefully arranged six or so separate rounded portions that are presented like table settings, one per seat, along with a rolling pin and maybe a dough-cutter for each placing. This arrangement may appear organized and possibly attractive to children, but it is not conducive to negotiation and sharing.

In addition to rethinking standard practices, specific cooperative games and activities that require joint effort can be provided. Interestingly, the Piagetian constructivist ideas of George Forman and Fleet Hill (1980) contain many fascinating and accessible examples of activities that are deliberately structured to require collaboration and cooperation, although the collaborative element is not highlighted in their writing.

Underpinning and perhaps overriding these pragmatics is the philosophical orientation of the teaching team (Hill, 1994). Greenberg (1992a, 1992b) has suggested a Deweyian framework for engendering a democratic ethos in early childhood classrooms. She also describes a number of practical ways for implementing democratic practices within early childhood settings. These include involving children in the planning of special events, facilitating discussions and meetings that encourage all children to express their views and to respect those of others, encouraging children to negotiate solutions to problems and conflicts, and pairing children together so that they can support each other. Teachers working together in a cooperative situation (usually the case in New Zealand early childhood centers) need to be able to take the time to clarify their views and come to a consensus in the approaches to be adopted.

Teachers' expectations of cooperation will transfer to children (Goffin, 1987). These expectations can be made explicit through role play and stories that provide examples of and strategies for cooperation (Liu & Greathouse, 1992). Interactions between children create many opportunities to support the development of negotiation skills. Wichert (1989) describes three levels that range from initial adult direction, to adults providing support, to the final stage of children taking charge. Initially, the adult may have to help children define the problem and model appropriate language and strategies, but eventually children are able to negotiate their own mutually satisfying arrangements. A student teacher focusing on this area during a third-year practicum with 4-year-old children commented with surprise on the speed with which the children picked up negotiation skills to the point that adult facilitation was rarely required. According to Wichert, "negotiating learning in children is a prime example of the importance of process over product" (p. 58). The process of negotiating their way through the conflict is important for children, often even more so than the eventual solution (Liu & Greathouse, 1992). Katz (1984) also pointed out the range of potential learning outcomes, including coping skills, conversational skills, and social skills, that may arise from a skilled teacher's response to children's conflicts.

Sociodramatic play is a rich source of cooperative endeavor (Goffin, 1987), since in order to participate children must develop the ability to assume interdependent roles, to maintain a common script of typical roles in the social world, and to be sensitive to the complexities of relationships by communicating and negotiating (Shipley, 1993). It also can be problematic that certain play roles are privileged and powerful (Mac Naughton, 1993, 1994). In the interests of equity, teachers have a responsibility to monitor children's sociodramatic play and find ways to intervene when it becomes oppressive to participants (Mac Naughton, 1997), rather than allowing their uncritiqued pedagogic discourse to render them powerless (Walkerdine, 1990).

Teachers also can generate collectivist possibilities by asking themselves the following questions:

1. What were our own experiences, as children, of cooperative endeavor?
2. How can we find out about the collective/individualistic dynamic within different cultural groups with whom we may work in early childhood centers?
3. What are key requirements for early childhood educators in terms of developing a team approach and a philosophy for implementing a collective ethos within the center program?

FINAL THOUGHTS

Te Whāriki provides a framework for a socioculturally aware collectivist philosophy of early childhood pedagogy to be implemented in Aotearoa/New Zealand. This provides a refreshing counter to the previous legacy of individualistic New Right philosophies. However, the writers of the curriculum themselves have expressed concerns that without sufficient government commitment to ensure that the structural supports of adequate funding, quality staffing, and teacher education and qualification requirements are in place, the new curriculum will not be able to deliver on its potential to make a difference for children (May & Carr, 1997). With social and political support, early childhood educators have the potential to implement socially and culturally responsive programs that foster a sense of respect, caring, and community.

REFERENCES

Apple, M. (1998, April). Chair/discussant for the symposium, *Knowledge politics and multiculturalism discourse*, at the annual meeting of the American Educational Research Association, San Diego.

Broadhead, P. (1997). Promoting sociability and cooperation in nursery settings. *British Educational Research Journal, 23*(4), 513–531.

Buck, P. (1958). *The coming of the Maori*. Wellington: Whitcombe and Tombs.

Carr, M., & May, H. (1993). Choosing a model. Reflecting on the development process of Te Whāriki: National Early Childhood Curriculum Guidelines in New Zealand. *International Journal of Early Years Education, 1*(3), 7–21.

Derman-Sparks, L. (1989). *Anti-bias curriculum: Tools for empowering young children*. Washington, DC: National Association for the Education of Young Children.

Dewey, J. (1966). *Democracy and education*. New York: Free Press.

Fay, B. (1987). *Critical social science*. Oxford: Polity Press.

Forman, G., & Hill, F. (1980). *Constructive play: Applying Piaget in the preschool*. Monterey, CA: Brooks/Cole.

Freire, P., & Shor, I. (1987). *A pedagogy for liberation: Dialogues on transforming education*. London: Macmillan.

Gardner, H. (1984). *Frames of mind: The theory of multiple intelligences*. London: Heinemann.

Gardner, H. (1998, April). *Where to draw the line: The perils of new para digms*. Presented at the annual meeting of the American Educational Research Association, San Diego.

Gerber, M. (Ed.). (1979). *The RIE manual: For parents and professionals*. Los Angeles: Resources for Infant Educarers.

Giroux, H. (1995). Series foreword. In J. Jipson, P. Munro, S. Victor, K. Jones, & G. Freed-Rowland (Eds.), *Repositioning feminism and education: Perspectives on educating for social change* (pp. ix–xi). Westport, CT: Bergin & Garvey.

Giroux, H. A., & McLaren, P. (1992). Writing from the margins: Geographies of identity, pedagogy, and power. *Journal of Education, 174*(1), 7–30.

Goffin, S. (1987, January). Cooperative behaviors: They need our support. *Young Children, 42*(3), 75–81.

Greenberg, P. (1992a). Ideas that work with young children: How to institute some simple democratic practices pertaining to respect, rights, roots and responsibilities in any classroom. *Young Children, 47*(5), 10–17.

Greenberg, P. (1992b). Why not academic preschool? (Part 2), Autocracy or democracy in the classroom. *Young Children, 47*(3), 54–64.

Hill, S. (1994). Cooperative communities in early childhood. *Australian Journal of Early Childhood, 19*(4), 44–48.

Jones, E., & Reynolds, G. (1992). *The play's the thing: Teachers' roles in children's play.* New York: Teachers College Press.

Katz, L. (1984, July). The professional early childhood teacher. *Young Children, 39*(1), 3–10.

Katz, L., & McClellan, D. (1991). *The teacher's role in the social development of young children.* University of Illinois: ERIC.

Kingsolver, B. (1993). *Pigs in heaven.* New York: Harper Perennial.

Leavitt, R., & Power, M. B. (1997). Civilizing bodies: Children in day care. In J. Tobin (Ed.), *Making a place for pleasure in early childhood education* (pp. 39–75). New Haven: Yale University Press.

Lindauer, S. (1987). Montessori education for young children. In J. Roopnarine & J. Johnson (Eds.), *Approaches to early childhood education* (pp. 109 –126). Columbus, OH: Merrill.

Liu, K., & Greathouse, N. (1992). Early experience of cooperative learning in preschool classrooms. *Contemporary Education, 63*(3), 195–200.

May, H., & Carr, M. (1997). Making a difference for the under fives? The early implementation of Te Whāriki, the New Zealand National Early Childhood Curriculum. *International Journal of Early Years Education, 5*(3), 225–232.

Mac Naughton, G. (1993). Gender, power and racism: A case study of domestic play in early childhood. *Multicultural Teaching, 11*(3), 12–15.

Mac Naughton, G. (1994). "You can be dad": Gender and power in domestic discourses and fantasy play within early childhood. *Journal for Australian Research in Early Childhood Education, 1*, 93–101.

Mac Naughton, G. (1997). Who's got the power? Rethinking gender equity strategies in early childhood. *International Journal of Early Years Education, 5*(1), 57–66.

McLaren, P. (1989). *Life in schools: An introduction to critical pedagogy in the foundations of education.* New York: Longman.

McLaren, P., & Leonardo, Z. (1998, April). *Epistemologies of whiteness.* Presented at the annual meeting of the American Educational Research Association, San Diego.

Ministry of Education. (1993). *The New Zealand curriculum framework.* Wellington: Author.

Ministry of Education. (1996). *Te Whāriki: He Whāriki Mātauranga mö ngä Mokopuna o Aotearoa: Early Childhood Curriculum.* Wellington: Learning Media.

Noddings, N. (1992). *The challenge to care in schools: An alternative approach to education.* New York: Teachers College Press.

Pihama, L. (1993). *Tungia te Ururua, Kia Tupu Whakaritorito te Tupu o te Harakeke: A critical analysis of parents as first teachers.* Unpublished master's thesis, Auckland University.

Polokow, V. (1992). *The erosion of childhood.* Chicago: University of Chicago Press.

Rogoff, B. (1990). *Apprenticeship in thinking.* New York: Oxford University Press.

Rogoff, B. (1991). The joint socialization of development by young children and adults. In M. Lewis & S. Feinman (Eds.), *Social influences and socialization in infancy* (pp. 253–280). New York: Plenum.

Shea, C. (1996). Critical and constructive post-modernism: The transformative power of holistic education. *Holistic Education Review, 9*(3), 40–49.

Shipley, D. (1993). *Empowering children: Play-based curriculum for lifelong learning.* Scarborough, ON: Nelson Canada.

Smith, A. (1993). Early childhood educare: Seeking a theoretical framework in Vygotsky's work. *International Journal of Early Years Education, 1*(1), 47–61.

Tangaere, A. R. (1997). *Te Kōhanga Reo: More than a language nest* (Early Childhood Folio 3—A Collection of Recent Research). Wellington: New Zealand Council for Educational Research.

Walkerdine, V. (1990). Sex, power and pedagogy. In *Schoolgirl fictions.* London: Verso.

Wichert, S. (1989). *Keeping the peace: Practicing cooperation and conflict resolution with preschoolers.* Philadelphia: New Society.

Youniss, J. (1994). Vygotsky's fragile genius in time and place. *Human Development, 37*, 119–124.

CHAPTER 10

Racial and Ethnic Mirrors: Reflections on Identity and Voice from an Asian American Educator

Susan Matoba Adler

AS A JAPANESE AMERICAN scholar-educator, I examine ethnic culture and critical race theory to attempt to connect them with Asian and Pacific American teacher identity and voice. We all see ourselves through racial and ethnic mirrors, a reflection of our self-constructed and appropriated identities, and we teach through our cultural lenses, which reflect and give voice to our values, beliefs, and world views. My own identity was profoundly affected by my participation in the conference on reconceptualizing early childhood education held in Honolulu, Hawai'i, in 1998. The very process of interacting professionally and personally, and the sharing of individual responses to significant events at the conference, created a discourse for reconceptualizing early childhood teacher identity and voice. Each participant went to the conference with perspectives on his or her own research and assumptions about its significance, and left with a richer understanding of how that frame of reference might be interpreted differently by other scholars.

I went to Honolulu with a perspective on Asian panethnicity, my own sense of racial and ethnic identity, and my experiences as an Asian American educator in the predominantly European American Midwest. In Hawai'i, I entered a sociocultural context of White and Japanese American political dominance. My previously held conception of Asian American oppression, where a segregated Black–White dichotomy renders Asians somewhat invisible, was challenged. The rich cultural connections I made at the conference with native Hawai'ians, Japanese Americans, Chinese from Hong Kong, Chinese and Vietnamese Americans from New York City, and Mäori from New Zealand overwhelmed me with a sense of Asian and Pacific Islander panethnicity that stretched beyond my midwestern roots.

GOING TO HAWAI'I: AN ETHNIC IDENTITY EXPERIENCE

Through interactions several years earlier with Joe Tobin, of the University of Hawai'i, I was mentally prepared for my experience in Hawai'i. When I was a graduate student, I shared my dissertation topic on the views and ethnic identity of midwestern Japanese American women with Joe. He listened intently, then pointed out that it was only on the "mainland" that Asian Americans were concerned about constructing their ethnic identity. Hawai'ians were used to a multitude of Asian ethnicities and had been acculturated over the generations. Japanese Americans, according to Takaki (1989, 1993), faced some discrimination on Hawai'ian plantations but had not been interned, or politically segregated, like those of Japanese heritage on the West Coast during World War II. The hierarchy of Japanese American dominance in Hawai'ian institutions had escaped my consideration, as did the plight of native Hawai'ians in their own homeland. When I later visited Hawai'i for the reconceptualizing conference, I brought a sense of cultural affinity that I had learned from my study participants, some of whom had grown up in the Midwest and migrated to communities in California with large Asian American populations. While I was on the "islands," much happened in terms of my racial and ethnic awareness, which I shared with Gail Nomura, a Japanese American from Hawai'i and assistant professor at the University of Washington. Her appraisal of the difference between mainland and Hawai'ian Asian Americans was much like Joe Tobin's.

Upon arriving in Hawai'i, I began to make mental notes of my experiences. A military man in the seat next to me told me about his Chinese wife and biracial children. I saw lots of Asians ("Orientals") as I walked through the airport. Rice and teriyaki were served at the dinner buffet at Tokai University. There were many tourists from Japan at the Japanese-owned Pacific Beach Hotel. Some proprietors at the hotel shops spoke Japanese to me, while Polynesian and Hawai'ian personnel in the hotel restaurant assumed that I was from Hawai'i.

(They knew that I wasn't like the tourists from Japan, but were surprised that I was a Midwesterner.) Where I strolled between the hotel and conference center, there were lots of Japanese and Asian shops and restaurants. And, as expected, most of the conference participants were European American, except for a handful of Asian Americans and the native Hawai'ian students. Later, I met Charles Araki, the Interim Dean of the College of Education at the University of Hawai'i at Manoa. I was surprised, since there are so few Sansei, or third-generation Japanese Americans like myself, in powerful administrative positions. Feelings of ethnic affiliation and a comfort level of seeing myself, an Asian American, in the population were beginning to emerge. I was not the invisible minority that I was accustomed to being.

BEGINNING THE DIALOGUE: ASIAN PANETHNICITY

I arrived at the conference intending to share my research agenda on the racial and ethnic socialization of Asian American and multiracial children. The focus was to be on how these identities are constructed and appropriated (Root, 1992; Thornton, 1992) and the dilemma surrounding stereotyping and using a color-blind orientation to teaching young children (Nieto, 1996; Paley, 1989). I wanted to compare how Asian American families socialized their children regarding race and ethnicity within the teacher/school approaches to multicultural and anti-bias education (Banks, 1994; Derman-Sparks, 1989; Sleeter & Grant, 1994). I wanted to dialogue with others about how ethnicity and culture could be preserved, if desired, but, more crucially, how we help children negotiate the inequities and discrimination they may face, without understanding the nature of racial segregation. Parents and teachers need, I believe, to critically examine the political and historical issues surrounding the panethnic movement, in order to socialize their children to confront, rather than ignore, racism. They need to directly address racial inequality and our status as invisible minorities and advocate for their children through political activism or creative endeavors such as writing books for children with relevant Asian American themes.

Panethnicity, as described by Espiritu (1992), refers to "the generalization of solidarity among ethnic sub-groups" (p. 6). Each Asian ethnic group has a unique cultural system, but we all face categorization or "lumping" into one group in a race-conscious American society. The primordialist approach to theories of ethnicity relies on "communities of culture" that help us acquire skills to negotiate within our cultural group, and help others recognize cultural differences. The instrumentalist approach to ethnicity, with its emphasis on "communities of interest," brings us together in order to share common concerns (Lee, 1996). We are often the recipients of inequitable treatment, and these approaches could provide mechanisms for structurally challenging the way Asian and Pacific Americans are represented.

For my conference presentation I shared a diagram illustrating the interrelationships among teacher lenses (how teachers perceived Asian American students), parent lenses (how parents understand and socialize their children), and the Asian American student/child's lens and mirror of self-identity. Each lens represented points of a triangle.

We discussed ideas like teachers and parents viewing the Asian or Pacific American child through their own cultural lenses and attempting to inculcate the beliefs and values of their own culture. When the teacher is a female from a middle-class European American background, that can lead to a cultural mismatch between her and the Asian American students in her class. Teachers, therefore, need to become cognizant of the nature of this mismatch and strive to gain cultural knowledge from parents.

In the process of constructing his or her own racial and ethnic identity, the child absorbs and then reflects the parental and school cultural norms and expectations. Teachers and parents reciprocate, cognizant of their own lenses and agendas for socializing the child, in order to monitor educational progress and maintain cultural congruency. They develop mutual respect as they build rapport that will support the child's academic success. If teachers and parents also take time to self-reflect, they too will discover mirrors of racial and ethnic identity. Asian American children, who are struggling to process divergent or conflicting cultural messages from parents and teachers, might have to choose between asserting themselves as individuals in schools or conforming to the group to maintain harmony within the family. This confusion can lead to what Sue (1973) referred to as the "marginal man."

European American teachers, particularly in the Midwest, may view their Asian American students through cultural lenses formed by their own limited experiences with people of color, stereotypes like the "model minority" (Lee, 1996; Osajima, 1987; Suzuki, 1977), and a color-blind perspective, which focuses on overlooking racial differences. Asian American parents and parents of children adopted from Asia may subscribe to a color-blind, assimilationist position, or they may inculcate Asian cultural values of collectivism and reverence for family and elders along with Western values of independence and individualism (Kitano & Daniels, 1988; Suzuki, 1980). However, embedded in these mirrors and lenses are levels of expectations for student/ child behavior and achievement that are reinforced by dominant White societal norms. In Tai's (1998) concept of negative reciprocity, the destructive nature of White support for the model minority myth serves as a normative tool for the perpetuation of White racial ideology. Could the socialization of Asian American children as respectful, hardworking, high achievers actually reify White domination? My paradigm provides a plausible pathway for intercultural understanding, but the message could as easily be one of assimilation, as well as one of pluralism. The color blindness that I wished to problematize could still be reflected in the mirrors of self-definition.

As the conference session evolved, the original intent of examining ethnic identity formation, panethnicity, and the socialization of young children began to change with participants sharing their stories of racial and ethnic awareness and oppression. Issues of "voice" from marginalized ethnic groups began to emerge, especially and powerfully from the native Hawai'ian and Mäori women. I had met some of the Mäori women and listened to their beliefs about their culture of collectivism, without considering their minority-group status. I lived in my own ethnocentric state of being, while assuming that I could intellectually embrace multiple perspectives on race and ethnicity. I needed to release myself from the quiet, neutral, nonconfrontational cultural stance from which I was socialized and seriously examine how critical race theory intersects with or conflicts with theories of ethnicity. How do appropriated messages about race and ethnicity inform the personal construction of racial and ethnic identity? As participants began sharing their stories, the focus of the session began to shift from the socialization of students to the identity formation and quest for "voice" of Asian American teachers.

VOICES THAT CHALLENGED MY ETHNOCENTRICITY

Ladson-Billings and Tate (1995) maintain that social reality is constructed by the formation and exchange of stories by people of color serving as interpretive structures and providing "psychic preservation of marginalized groups" (p. 56). At the conference, when Kerri-Ann Hewitt asked, "Can I be myself, be Hawai'ian, and be a teacher?" and spoke of feeling marginalized in a school of education headed by a Japanese American like myself, I felt a pang of sadness in discovering that my ethnic group could represent oppressors. I speak not of the individual (Dean Araki, in particular), but of institutional racism embedded in universities and public policy. I began to understand how some of my midwestern education students feel when I use the internment of Japanese Americans as an example of historical racism, causing them to grapple with the possibility of their own White privilege. My reality had been challenged by Kerri-Ann's story of her reality. By most accounts, I am a confident, competent human being, a Japanese American woman who is a highly educated professional. This experience caused me to reflect upon what personal and political costs I endured to become what I am.

Later during the presentation, when the Maori educators, Margaret Nicholls, Jenny Ritchie, Rita Walker, and Amiria O'Malley, rose to chant a response of appreciation and connectedness to the words of the Hawai'ian presenters, my own sense of the dichotomous relationship between victim and oppressor was awakened. Panel members Kerri-Ann Hewitt, Julie Thirugnanam, Donna Grace, and Joe Tobin shared that dynamic moment of condemnation for colonial oppression with everyone in the room. Perhaps the impact was more salient for those of us in the audience who were Asian, Asian and Pacific American, Māori, and native Hawai'ian, for in our diverse ways we each have experienced oppression. But those who oppose inequity in our society, and in public institutions like universities and schools, could empathize and share in the moment of raw emotion.

For me, this act of solidarity was *the* defining moment of the conference because I connected with the part of me that had been repressed as a Japanese American growing up in the Midwest during the post-World War II years. In my family, we never outwardly acknowledged our race, ethnicity, or culture. Our Japanese identities were always silenced at school, at home, and in the small Japanese American community where grandparents got together to speak Japanese and to play Hana, a Japanese card game. Our Nisei parents chose assimilation into the dominant European American culture for us; we wholeheartedly internalized and appropriated that identity. Being visibly Asian was problematic enough in terms of peer socialization, so we did not want to "act Japanese" or call attention to our home culture.

At this conference session, in this time and space of personal awareness, I also experienced a profound sense of "family comfort" from two young Asian Americans that I had just met. Regina Chiou, a second-grade teacher from New York City, and Lamson Lam, a graduate student at New York University, gave me emotional support, sharing my sense of Asian identity. It was an awesome experience to hear the words of the Hawai'i panel, embrace the Māori response, and then, through my profuse tears, listen to Regina and Lamson tell of their ethnic and racial awareness. Regina instinctively put her arms around me, as a daughter would comfort a distressed mother. Lamson thoughtfully brought us all refreshments, fruit and drinks, as my teenaged son would do for his mother when she needs nourishment. Then, Lamson shared his heartfelt response to Julie Thirugnanam's research on the effervescent "aloha spirit," which has roots in White oppression. He recalled how he had been socialized into projecting that same facade, having grown up biracial, Caucasian and Vietnamese Hawai'ian. His conflicting bicultural world of upper-class White privilege, the poverty of the inner-city children with whom he worked, and his Asian American rearing in Hawai'i were creating a dissonance he had not voiced before. I was emotionally drained and intellectually enriched.

TEACHERS AND RACIAL/ETHNIC AWARENESS

Returning to the interrelationships of teacher, parent, and child cultural lenses, I would like to focus on the teacher's racial, ethnic, and cultural awareness. Teachers seek information from both parents and the children in their classes about their lives, beliefs, and experiences, then reflect back to each through their own cultural lenses. The lenses reflect the teachers' own cultural awareness, race, class, gender, ethnicity, religion, and belief systems. Asian American teachers, drawing from their own cultural background, might have high expectations for their students in terms of behavior and effort (Adler, 1998; Stevenson, 1992). To illustrate, for Japanese American teachers, the expectation for students would be to "do your best" and maintain task persistence at all times, putting emphasis on the process of learning rather than on a product such as a high grade or tangible reward (Adler, 1998).

Before I went to Hawai'i, my racial, ethnic, and cultural lenses reflected my life experiences as a visible minority, with little access to an ethnic community, in a European American middle-class society. I held a weak ethnic and racial identity and used my own cultural background as merely supplementary knowledge for teaching in both public schools and at the university level. I taught units on Japan and Japanese culture, I introduced the internment of Japanese Americans during World War II to students in my multicultural education classes, and I supported multicultural and ethnic study initiatives. But I did not see my teaching as a reflection of me as a Japanese American woman. Why would I be different from most of the European American students who shared my teacher training programs? I learned to implement pedagogy and select curriculum without regard to the cultural context of my students' or my own life. I wasn't cognizant of how my interpretation of curriculum and my pedagogic style were filtered through and shaped by my Asian American cultural lens.

This perspective changed after my personal experiences in Hawai'i because my sense of racial and ethnic identity changed. I became cognizant of how my philosophy of education was shaped by my bicultural value system, my reticent Japanese American interactional style, and my relativistic approach to dichotomous Western education. This change, of course, did not happen over night. My experiences in Hawai'i solidified what I had been processing as an educator over many years as a classroom teacher, a graduate student, and a professor.

ASIAN/PACIFIC AMERICAN TEACHER IDENTITY AND VOICE

As educators, we can become the conduit to a more sensitive and equitable multicultural society of the future. We should be carefully investing in the culturally diverse student population of today, preparing students to recognize and appreciate the cultural lenses of others, and encouraging them to share perspectives, unite, and speak in one voice. Stacey Lee's (1996) ethnography of high school Asian American students describes various Asian ethnic groups, illustrating how alliances can, but may not always, be made among the groups. Asian American educators might see themselves as a catalytic force that stimulates the development of ethnic and racial self-identity, that teaches the purpose and political advantage of panethnicity, and that nurtures individuals to express themselves so that their voices will not be silenced. We need to instill the value of dialogue about race and ethnicity, while eradicating the often-cited "fear of offending," which plagues open, honest, cross-cultural, interracial communication.

Racial integration in U.S. public schools, despite its historical and political significance, brought people of color together in artificial situations, reinforced the color-blind philosophy, and eventually led to informal re-segregation. Multicultural education, despite the groundbreaking efforts to create equal educational opportunities and mutual understanding, led to the proliferation of difference, tension among groups, and a superficial "unity of difference" (Ladson-Billings & Tate, 1995). Where, then, should Asian and Pacific American teachers turn for philosophical guidance? Perhaps, critical race theory as applied to education, and panethnicity, as unified voice, could provide the grounding for future research. Ladson-Billings and Tate (1995) explain:

The "voice" component of critical race theory provides a way to communicate the experience and realities of the oppressed, a first step on the road to justice. As we attempt to make linkages between critical race theory and education, we contend that the voice of people of color is required for a complete analysis of the educational system. . . . Thus, without authentic voices of people of color (as teachers, parents, administrators, students, and community members) it is doubtful that we can say or know anything useful about education in their communities. (p. 58)

In closing, I return to my experiences in Hawai'i, this time at the Hawai'ian immersion school in Honolulu. As we entered, Hawai'ian children were teaching the other visitors an authentic Hawai'ian hula, not the tourist version commonly performed on Waikiki Beach. They were representing their home culture with their delightful voices and rhythmic movements. The classroom walls were filled with symbols of their native language, words unfamiliar to our mainland ears. Their competent bilingual teachers were making learning culturally relevant by teaching through their native language and infusing their own cultural understandings with new information. As we observed through our own cultural lenses, I couldn't help hiding my elation, knowing that those Hawai'ian parents, teachers, and children were defining themselves in their mirrors, rather than appropriating the identities assigned to them by others. This school represented a safe place, in a public institution, where students, parents, and teachers had personal and political voice and where their culture was affirmed rather than silenced.

REFERENCES

Adler, S. M. (1998). *Mothering, education, and ethnicity: The transformation of Japanese American culture.* New York: Garland.

Banks, J. (1994). *An introduction to multicultural education.* Boston: Allyn & Bacon.

Derman-Sparks, L. (1989). *Anti-bias curriculum: Tools for empowering young children.* Washington, DC: National Association for the Education of Young Children.

Espiritu, Y. L. (1992). *Asian American panethnicity: Bridging institutions and identities.* Philadelphia: Temple University Press.

Kitano, H. L., & Daniels, B. (1988). *Asian Americans: Emerging minorities.* Englewood Cliffs, NJ: Prentice-Hall.

Ladson-Billings, G., & Tate, W. F. (1995). Toward a critical race theory of education. *Teachers College Record, 97,* 47–68.

Lee, S. J. (1996). *Unraveling the "model minority" stereotype: Listening to Asian American youth.* New York: Teachers College Press.

Nieto, S. (1996). *Affirming diversity: The sociopolitical context of multicultural education* (2nd ed.). White Plains, NY: Longman.

Osajima, K. (1987). Asian Americans as the model minority: An analysis of the popular press image in the 1960's and 1980's. In G. Y. Okihiro (Ed.), *Reflections on shattered windows: Promises and prospects for Asian American studies* (pp. 165–174). Pullman: Washington State University Press.

Paley, V. (1989). *White teacher.* Cambridge, MA: Harvard University Press.

Root, M. P. (1992). Loyalty, rootedness and belonging: The quest for defining Asian American identity. In L. C. Lee (Ed.), *Asian Americans: Collages of identities* (pp. 175–183). Ithaca, NY: Cornell University Press.

Sleeter, C., & Grant, C. (1994). *Making choices for multicultural education: Five approaches to race, class, and gender* (2nd ed.). New York: Macmillan.

Stevenson, H. W. (1992, December). Learning from Asian schools. *Scientific American*, pp. 70–76.

Sue, S. (1973). Ethnic identity: The impact of two cultures on the psychological development of Asian Americans. In S. Sue & N. Wagner (Eds.), *Asian American psychological perspectives* (pp. 140–149). Palo Alto, CA: Science and Behavior Books.

Suzuki, B. H. (1977). Education and socialization of Asian Americans: A revisionist analysis of the "model minority" thesis. *Amerasia Journal, 4,* 23–52.

Suzuki, B. H. (1980). The Asian American family. In M. D. Fantini & R. Cardenas (Eds.), *Parenting in a multicultural society* (pp. 74–102). New York: Longman.

Tai, R. H. (1998). [Review of *The politics of racial identity: A pedagogy of invisibility*]. *Educational Researcher, 27,* 36–40.

Takaki, R. (1989). *Strangers from a different shore: A history of Asian Americans.* Boston: Little, Brown.

Takaki, R. (1993). *A different mirror: A history of multicultural America.* Boston: Little, Brown.

Thornton, M. (1992). Finding a way home: Race, nation and sex in Asian American identity. In L. C. Lee (Ed.), *Asian Americans: Collages of identities* (pp. 165–174). Ithaca, NY: Cornell University Press.

CHAPTER 11

Postcolonial Ethnography, Young Children, and Voice

Radhika Viruru & Gaile S. Cannella

AS ACADEMICS, we are aware of at least two interpretations of the term *postcolonial*. One was voiced by Alma Ata Aidoo (1991): "Applied to Africa, India, and some other parts of the world, 'postcolonial' is not only a fiction, but a most pernicious fiction, a cover-up of a dangerous period in our peoples' lives" (p. 152). Aidoo and others are concerned that the use of the prefix *post* implies the end of a colonial period and denies present economic, political, and discursive inequities. The second interpretation reads the prefix *post* as representing both the end of colonialisms in which land and people were physically appropriated, and the continued effects of colonizing power through discursive practices and philosophical domination. This perspective would deconstruct European thought, critiquing systems of power and knowledge (Mongia, 1996). The dialogue between the two views reveals the possibility that, although postcolonial theory may illuminate dominant narratives, the discourse also can serve to reinforce existing power structures (Coronil, 1992; Dirlik, 1994; Jacoby, 1995). From within this context, and recognizing the possibility that all constructions generate multiple sites of power, we attempt to critique from a postcolonial perspective the notion of research, especially ethnographic research, as applied to young children.

WHO ARE WE TO SPEAK!?

We begin by explaining who we are at the moment of our critique. What gives us the right to speak of postcolonial, of ethnography, of those who are younger? With whose voices do we speak? Do we represent the colonizer, the colonized, both, or neither? We struggle to determine the nature of our voices. Do we speak as one, or dialogically as two, or is human communication more complex, perhaps ambiguous? Finally, we decide that neither of us has one voice; neither is separate from the influence of the other or the multiple voices and discourses that surround us. We will simply, although not accurately or easily, list some of the multiple selves that we have constructed and believe that our audience will recognize the complex, uncertain, and problematic nature of these selves.

> RADHIKA: My voices would be considered postcolonial. I was born in India in 1964, so colonization is not something that I have lived through. But, my father told me, his eyes shining, how the Union Jack came down for the first time in 200 years and the tri-colored Indian flag was raised on our "new" nation. So colonization is not very far either. My own encounters with colonization have been perhaps more postcolonial—trying as a woman, a person from the so-called "Third World," and as a mother, to find a space in overwhelmingly patriarchal and Western discourses.
>
> GAILE: My voices are typically American, educated, middle-class, and White. I feel that I have learned to speak as an adoptive mother of a child of color (a child from India), as a family member, and as a working woman (in a society that gives multiple contradictory messages to women about their roles). I understand those discourses to which Radhika refers, and sometimes I feel that I may perpetuate them because of my privileged White, middle-class status.

We are both early childhood educators, grounded in the developmental theory that has dominated the field. In recent years we have focused on the work of feminists of color, critical theorists, and various poststructuralists. Radhika's recent work with children and teachers in India has not only added to our belief in deconstruction and critique, but reinforced our concern for younger human beings as the unrestrictedly, yet invisibly, colonized.

RADHIKA: It was only when doing the background research for a
   lengthy ethnographic study of preschool in urban India, that
   is, my doctoral dissertation, that I became aware of the postcolonial movement. Suddenly, I was saddled with the title
   "postcolonial ethnographer" and was not quite sure what to
   do with the label. At times, quite unexpectedly, it seemed to
   fit rather well. When I returned home to India to do my research, both my children went with me; my son, then 4, and
   my daughter, then only 3 months old. One day as I was playing with my daughter, I found that one of the pet names I
   had for her was "bluest." As long as we were in India, I kept
   calling her that, but I could never really trace where that
   name came from. It was only when we returned to Texas
   that it hit me; it came from a country music song called
   "The Bluest Eyes in Texas." I was shocked. My daughter
   will never have the bluest eyes in Texas. On the other hand,
   she does not look very different from half the other children
   in Texas; indeed as many people tell me, she could very
   well be Hispanic. One never hears about the brownest eyes
   in Texas. It struck me then that colonization was not something that one had to go back home to seek; it was staring
   me right in the face in College Station, Texas.

This kind of colonization seems to be the most painful; it is no
longer about physical subjugation (a form that, however violent, is
open and obvious), but about all the things one cannot but, according
to a powerful Other, should be. Present-day postcolonial analysis requires that we first recognize the ways in which groups of people,
including those who are younger, are colonized through hidden messages about themselves. One dominant form of colonization is found
in the scientific construction of childhood as a predetermined universal truth, perspectives from which one group creates beliefs about and
values for the other.

THE UNIVERSAL CHILD: UNRESTRICTEDLY COLONIZED

Ariès (1962) proposed that before the "modern" period in Western Europe, notions of childhood as a distinct period of human development
did not exist. Following the Enlightenment, younger human beings
were constructed as separate from adults, as innocent and needing protection from the world, as incompetent, and as requiring guidance in

the control of their "savage" tendencies. Twenty years ago, Kessen (1979) demonstrated how different children were constructed by different theorists: for Freud, a being created through sexual desire; for Piaget, a creature of adaptation; and for Skinner, a "baby in a box" (p. 28). Other scholars have expanded this work through deconstruction and genealogy. The concept of child is found to clearly reflect Enlightenment/modernist discourses that perpetuate notions of (1) truth (as revealed in the existence of the child whose universal nature is considered predetermined), (2) positivist science (the authority used for surveillance and determination of this universal child), (3) Cartesian oppositional dichotomy (as reflected in adult/child characterizations of those who are intelligent, strong, mature, civilized, and in control as compared with those who are innocent, weak, immature, savage, and unrestrained), and (4) the belief in human progress (well illustrated in the psychological construction of human development), to name just a few. Although created in Europe and the United States by the Christian church as those needing protection from a corrupt society, and by the positivist science of psychology, the notion of the truth of childhood has been/is imposed on all younger human beings around the world, as well as so-called Western children (Cahan, Mechling, Sutton-Smith, & White, 1993; Cannella, 1997; Woodhead, 1990).

In addition to recent deconstructive challenges to the scientific understanding of younger human beings as "universal children," our constructions of childhood clearly can be analyzed from postcolonial perspectives. We briefly discuss two of these sources: (1) the scholarly work in postcolonial theory, and (2) constructions of childhood represented by those who have resisted colonial domination.

Postcolonial Theory

As are poststructuralists (Foucault, 1980) and feminists (Gordon, 1988; Spivak, 1996), postcolonial scholars are concerned with issues of discourse, agency, representation, identity, and history. Although critiqued for creating theories that "de-center the subject," Bhabha (1996) addresses the general way in which colonial discourses are used to construct the "Other" (p. 37). These conditions of colonial discourse also can be applied to the construction of the universal child. Colonization produces a "subject peoples" (p. 37) by creating knowledge about the people through surveillance. Authority is created over the subject peoples through the construction of two stereotyped groups, as if in opposition to each other. One group becomes the oppressed, the other the oppressor. The colonized subject peoples are described as lacking, as degenerate, which is the justification for control and the creation of administrative systems over them. Colonization of one group over the other is accepted as a fixed reality, as a necessary truth, and as the sign of stability and normalcy.

The universal child fits this description of the colonized Other. Children have been created as a group of people who must be observed and who are in opposition, at least in intellectual ability, agency, and behavior, to adults. Children represent a people who must be controlled and administered over until they progress developmentally, mature, and become self-disciplined. The truth of childhood is so accepted by adults that, except within the academy, there is no challenge. The signifiers of stability and normalcy are that adults take charge of children, administering and controlling their lives.

As discussed earlier, multiple concerns and perspectives are generated and problematized by postcolonial theorists. For example, using Foucault's work, Bhabha (1996) also decenters power relations, focusing on the notion that power (especially power that is not directly physical) is not dialectical. Power relations are not as simple as a dichotomy between self/other, oppressor/oppressed, or adult/child. Colonization cannot be subverted by simply being inverted. Children are not decolonized by simply being given power by adults. Spivak (1996) expresses another concern—that the Third World is being constructed by postcolonial theory as a new object of investigation. This concern also can be voiced regarding younger human beings. Postcolonial theory as applied to oppressed peoples, including children, can serve simply to create another avenue for academic research, a new way of legitimizing the construction of human beings as objects of our scientific inquiry. A final example is the concern with the increased use of postcolonial theory in defining marginal groups in the "First World" (Mongia, 1996, p. 6), an issue that would address diverse groups of children. This definition creates an ahistorical concept of power, reinforcing the Enlightenment/modernist notion of progress by defining periods as precolonial, colonial, and postcolonial. As postcolonial theory is applied to younger human beings, continual self-critique is obviously necessary to avoid inadvertently reproducing the colonizing discourses that we would challenge.

Alternative Constructions

Our present focus on India provides an example of the lives of younger human beings as not dominated by a construction of child that is separate from those who are older. Kumar (1993) cites a study of Indian childhood conducted by Lois Barclay Murphy in 1953. A certain "continuity" seemed to exist between the worlds of adults and children, a continuity in the sense of proximity. Kumar (1993) has interpreted this as meaning that "the child is seen as part of the adult space in daily life" (p. 66). During childhood, this continuity seemed to be expressed through close physical contact with the child, as children often were carried by adults as they went around their daily routines. In later years, this continuity continued, as children often were to be found in places where adults were talking or amusing themselves. This lack of separation and differentiation seemed to exist regardless of social class. Murphy contrasted this continuity of life experience with American practices of child rearing that are grounded in a philosophy of purposive upbringing, with the goals of autonomy and independence. One of Murphy's (1953) Indian informants is quoted as saying: "You bring up your children; we live with ours" (p. 66).

The adult/child continuity theme also is described in a study of Indian childhood by Anandalakshmy and Bajaj (1981). Working with a community of silk weavers, known as the Momin Ansaris, in Varanasi in North India, these researchers found that, in general, adults and children inhabited the same spaces. Children, like adults, dealt with a number of complex issues simultaneously. Human beings were not rigidly separated into children and adults.

Contradicting the notion of the universal child, Misri (1986) has argued that the notions of childhood in India that do exist seem to be constructed on three different "axes," which are composed of completely antithetical ideas. First, the child is seen to be simultaneously a creation of the parents and a gift from God, and is thus the axis of the human divine. Parents, from within this perspective, are simply instruments through whom the divine will is realized. The second axis brings together yet another set of opposing ideas: The child is simultaneously both a collective being and a unique individual. Hindu religious beliefs such as the concept of karma emphasize the actions an individual must take, while social relationships with the family and community stress collectivity. The third axis tries to reconcile the idea that a child is not a blank slate, but born with certain unalterable characteristics, with the equally potent idea that a child can be transformed by rituals. Grounded in contradictions, this paradigm presents a complex, alternative postcolonial picture, a perspective that challenges the positivist focus on human nature as progressing toward logical reasoning.

POSTCOLONIAL RESEARCH AND CHILDREN

Research, from a postcolonial perspective, is recognized as a European American discursive practice that constructs colonizing power for one group over the other. In many ways, research is putting into practice the Enlightenment belief that truth, reason, and science are the paths to liberation, that knowledge is the savior of the world. Research is used to legitimate and justify actions over colonized peoples, whether the subject peoples are from a faraway land, neighbors of color, or people who are younger than we are. Radhika's work in India illustrates this issue:

> My ethnographic study was conducted in a small nursery school, serving about 115 children in the heart of the city of Hyderabad, a major city in Southern India. When I initially went there several years ago, although most people in the school were perfectly hospitable, their general attitude to my research can be summed up as a rather doubtful, "Why?" One day as I sat on the playground taking notes, one of the ayahs (aides) demanded to know why I would take notes on children's play; in further amazement, she wanted to know who was paying my salary. "Who on earth would pay one to do such a thing?" A traditional interpretation of this encounter could be to say that the woman was too poor and/or too uneducated to understand the importance of researching children's behavior—and she was both poor and uneducated. However, as I got to know her, I came to understand that she was expressing her amazement that one needed to do things like take notes to understand behavior. Further, she had a major problem with the idea that children had to be studied—like a subspecies.

Ethnography

Constructed as the "work of describing culture" (Spradley, 1980, p. 3), ethnography is perhaps the most widely used form of research with people who historically have been colonized and/or labeled savage or the "wretched of the earth" (Fanon, 1963). Although the definition of ethnography has generated controversy, ethnography is generally accepted as a form of social research that explores the nature of phenomena (rather than testing hypotheses), uses unstructured data, investigates cases in detail, and interprets the meaning of human action (Atkinson & Hammersley, 1994). Since the method appears to challenge the positivist focus on predetermination, experimental control, and researcher domination, ethnography has been adopted in a variety of fields concerned with the everyday lives and real-world practices of human beings. For years, ethnography has dominated the field of anthropology and recently has been accepted as the ideal method for conducting educational research with children in homes, communities, and schools.

Various scholars, especially feminists, critical theorists, and postmodernists, for some time have criticized ethnography as actually embodying hierarchical, undemocratic, colonizing practices. The researcher is considered to hold all the power, deciding who and what to study, and how the voices of others will be recorded and represented (Gitlin, Siegel, & Boru, 1989). An expanded criticism that is especially relevant to postcolonial issues is the nature of the narrative found in typical anthropological ethnographies; rather than diverse forms of reporting that could emerge from the vast array of human societies, the ethnographic monograph imposes a common textual pattern on all those who are "studied" (Boon, 1993). Ethnography has been critiqued as "fiction," a story constructed by the authors and shaped by the conventional practices of qualitative research and narrative production (Clifford & Marcus, 1986). Clough (1992, 1993) has even questioned the notion of experience, proposing that it is always constructed through discourse.

Early childhood educators have addressed similar issues by calling attention to the voyeuristic nature of participant-observation (Tobin & Davidson, 1990), the ethical paradox of intervention when involved in naturalistic inquiry (Hatch, 1995), the use of positivist reliability methods like triangulation (Walkerdine, 1997), and the researcher's perceived right to conduct surveillance on other people (Walkerdine, 1984). The latitude allowed in the construction and emergence of qualitative research masks the underlying assumptions that are imposed by the discourses of research and the academy. As an example, Radhika writes in field notes:

> There were times when I found the need to impose order on my data as constricting to the preschool in which I worked. Order, at times, seemed to be a very colonial idea. (The need to impose order on unenlightened masses was one of the strongest arguments in favor of the Empire.) When I asked the principal how she planned for teaching, she said that they just "got into a rhythm and did it." Possibly this would have been the Indian way to conduct my study. Possibly it would have been the respondents' own way of telling their story—but I found myself unable to relinquish ideas like order and categories of data. I would become

aware that what might be categories for me were not for my people.

Addressing these postmodern and postcolonial criticisms, anthropologists like Margery Wolf (1992) have responded with the belief that although ethnography has the potential for further colonization, the practice has revealed voices of the ignored and the silenced around the world. Referring to her own work, she states: "When I began my research, there were no Taiwanese scholars who were the least bit interested in women's lives. I may not have always gotten it right, but Taiwanese women were taken seriously as agents because of my research and writing" (p. 14).

Voice

Some feminists and critical theorists are exploring ways to conduct ethnography while simultaneously critiquing their own ethnographic projects. For example, feminist ethnographers address the issue of voice, demonstrating that the modes of inquiry constructed through social science are both hierarchical and patriarchal and have ignored the voices of women and persons of color (Olesen, 1994). We would add the voices of children to this list of those who have been and are disregarded. Recent work does, however, explore unthought-of ways to expand the notion of research to diverse voices. As examples, Ruth Behar (1993) presents a double-voiced text, representing two voices simultaneously. Patti Lather's (1997) work has involved the continued examination of ways that women with HIV/AIDS can control and name their role in the research activity. Since in recent history adults have always spoken for children, the issue of voice is of major concern for ethnographic research in early childhood education.

Although concepts like "coming to voice," "polyvocality," and "hearing the voices of others" would appear to be ideal in a postcolonial project that would deconstruct systems of power and domination, the notion of voice is a complex, troublesome issue. In *Disruptive Voices*, Michelle Fine (1992) problematizes the concept as epistemologically inaccurate. First, researchers choose pieces of narrative (just as we have done for this chapter) that illustrate their own beliefs and agendas. Second, individual voices are taken as representations of group behavior, a clearly postcolonial issue. Finally, we as researchers often privilege contradictory, subjugated voices and reproduce their contents as free of power relations. As Foucault (1980) argued, "All voices contain and negotiate power relations. Oppressed informants are neither 'free' from nor uncontaminated by dominant perspectives" (p. 219). What is heard from others are often "ruling class scripts" (p. 216), the expression of critique and challenge being risky activities when one does not hold the power.

We would add further questions concerning the notion of voice as human representation. Is the concept one that actually perpetuates dominant views of the world? It appears individualistic and dangerously close to the gendered expectation that one would "standup for himself." What of forms of communication that do not fit European American constructions of direct talk? Postmodern ethnographers have pointed, for example, to the gender of the interviewer and the respondent as a filter of knowledge (Denzin, 1989). Feminists have even grown reluctant to interview other women, an activity that is believed to create them as objects, and have chosen to develop human relationships instead (Fontana & Frey, 1994; Reinharz, 1992). Finally, what of the power of silence? The discourse on voice negates the multiple directions of silence. As examples, multiple messages may be included in silence; a form of learning may occur through silence; silence may be resistance. Consider another illustration from Radhika's work in India:

One day in the upper kindergarten classroom, I witnessed the teacher showing the children the uses of the articles *a* and *an*. Although she gave them examples of how they were used, she did not tell them that *an* was to be used if the first letter was a vowel. The rule was implied and illustrated by the examples but not spoken aloud. This was very typical of an environment where things were rarely expressed directly. When the teachers read stories to the children, even tales with explicit moral messages about behavior, they were not openly discussed. However, the children were still expected to understand this on their own. The activities remind me of Trawick's (1990) description of interactions with a South Indian family. Ideas that were important were rarely said aloud, but were expected to be understood. This habit of not saying things aloud, of communicating through silence, was a pervasive part of the school atmosphere. The general attitude seemed to be that sincere feelings are demeaned when they are expressed openly.

The above issues regarding voice are obviously relevant for our work with those who are younger. Are there ways to hear the voices of children, to regard them as human beings, without imposing our expectations or our agendas on them? Do we have the right to question, observe, and interpret them? How do our methods create those who are younger as objects of colonizing power? What of silence? Do we place too much emphasis on oral and behavioral expression? Even when we have the best of intentions, how do our attempts to hear children serve as colonization? Are there ways that those of us who want to work with other human beings can learn to know each other without inadvertently working as colonizers?

RECONCEPTUALIZING RESEARCH: POSTCOLONIAL ALTERNATIVES

As anyone functioning from a postmodernist perspective would agree, we do not and cannot have the right answers for the construction of research that would not colonize children. We offer here some possibilities for reconceptualization. One possibility is that research can be viewed as a process of continual self-conscious critique. The work of criticalists and feminists that would examine the social and political forces influencing participants, researcher, and methods of inquiry illustrates this self-conscious functioning. The research of Richard Johnson (1997) and Mary Hauser (1995) provide examples.

Another related possibility is to radically change the research questions that we ask. Rather than assuming that the lives of others should be researched, we could address issues that reflect the social, political, and even educational context in which children live. The following are examples:

- "What are the ways in which early childhood curriculum reflects imperialist assumptions about and misrepresentations of historically colonized peoples?" (Cannella & Bailey, 1999, p. 23)
- "How do methods of screening, assessment, testing, and/or categorization of young children perpetuate the economic and social stratification of historically colonized peoples?" (Cannella & Bailey, 1999, p. 23)
- How does one co-construct a new kind of research with children that reflects their perspectives?
- Children might construct research very differently, in ways that do not fit traditional academic discourse. Where is the space for these "alternative" visions? Why must they be alternative?

A further possibility would be to reconceptualize the entirety of research, laying bare all research issues (e.g., problem definition, data collection, interpretation) in the construction of open community work. This type of research is partially displayed by Jipson and Paley in *Daredevil Research* (1997) and in the literacy teaching of Paulo Freire. This type of research requires full partnerships with community members, which in our case would be children. These community members would have equal, and perhaps greater, access to decisions regarding the entire process and forms of representation. Another example is found in Dyson's (1997) attempts to reconceptualize her ways of doing research. She describes how she co-constructed a role for herself with the children in her study of children "writing superheroes." Dyson found that she relied greatly on the goodwill and legitimacy conferred on her by the children, especially two children who were too involved with their own work to let her interfere. She further relates that only after establishing intimacy and becoming friends with the children, could she ask them questions about complex issues like race and gender. To have done so prematurely would have been impertinent. Such questions can be asked only within the boundaries of friendship. Dyson further acknowledges that if the children had control over the end product, it probably would not have been a book.

Finally, a postcolonial analysis would not be complete without the recommendation that research that constructs other human beings as objects be eliminated from our academic and educational practices. Can research ever be acceptable to those who have never had a role in its construction and only a limited role in influencing its results? Perhaps scholarly work becomes something different than the imposition of our practices on others.

Those of us who call ourselves educators/researchers (especially teacher educators) can use the multiple perspectives generated by postcolonial theories to:

1. Examine our dominant discourses, ways of functioning with others (e.g., young children, preservice teachers, inservice teachers, other researchers), and the institutionalized messages that further colonize, treating human beings as without agency or voice
2. Recognize that research (even qualitative, ethnographic research) is a form of Enlightenment/modernist colonization that must be deconstructed, turned upside down, perhaps rejected, and at least reconceptualized and reconstructed

We cannot complete this chapter without a final request regarding children. Since the adult/child dichotomy is perhaps the major colonizing force in the lives of younger human beings, we would suggest that those of us who share our lives with them make every effort to eliminate the dichotomy and the notion of the universal child. Only when we accept those who are younger as equal human beings with agency and power, will we begin to address our colonizing practices over them. Questions (like those presented throughout this chapter) must be asked and answered continually and actions taken. Actions must include the ways in which we conceptualize programs, the knowledge(s) that are considered important for ourselves and our students, and the decisions made for educational research and practice with children.

REFERENCES

Aidoo, A. A. (1991). That capacious topic: Gender politics. In P. Mariani (Ed.), *Critical fictions: The politics of imaginative writing* (pp. 151–154). Seattle: Bay Press.

Anandalakshmy, S., & Bajaj, M. (1981). Childhood in the weavers' community in Varanasi. In D. Sinha (Ed.), *Socialization of the Indian child* (pp. 31–38). New Delhi: Concept.

Ariès, P. (1962). *Centuries of childhood—A social history of family life.* New York: Knopf.

Atkinson, P., & Hammersley, M. (1994). Ethnography and participant observation. In N. Denzin & Y. Lincoln (Eds.), *Handbook of qualitative research* (pp. 248–261). Thousand Oaks, CA: Sage.

Behar, R. (1993). *Translated woman: Crossing the border with Esperanza's story.* Boston: Beacon.

Bhabha, H. (1996). The other question. In P. Mongia (Ed.), *Contemporary postcolonial theory: A reader* (pp. 37–54). London: Arnold.

Boon, J. A. (1993). Functionalists write too: Frazer, Malinowski and the semiotics of the monograph. *Semiotica, 46,* 131–149.

Cahan, E., Mechling, J., Sutton-Smith, B., & White, S. H. (1993). The elusive historical child: Ways of knowing the child of history and psychology. In G. H. Elder, Jr., J. Model, & R. D. Parke (Eds.), *Children in time and place: Developmental and historical insights* (pp. 192–223). New York: Cambridge University Press.

Cannella, G. S. (1997). *Deconstructing early childhood education: Social justice and revolution.* New York: Peter Lang.

Cannella, G. S., & Bailey, C. D. (1999). Postmodern research in early childhood education. In S. Reifel (Ed.), *Advances in early education and day care* (Vol. 10, pp. 3–39). Greenwich, CT: JAI Press.

Clifford, J., & Marcus, G. E. (Eds.). (1986). *Writing culture: The poetics and politics of ethnography.* Berkeley: University of California Press.

Clough, P. T. (1992). *The end(s) of ethnography: From realism to social criticism.* Newbury Park, CA: Sage.

Clough, P. T. (1993). On the brink of deconstructing sociology: A critical reading of Dorothy Smith's standpoint epistemology. *Sociology Quarterly, 34,* 169–182.

Coronil, F. (1992, Fall). Can postcoloniality be decolonized? Imperial banality and postcolonial power. *Public Culture,* p. 5.1.

Denzin, N. K. (1989). *Interpretive interactionism.* Newbury Park, CA: Sage.

Dirlik, A. (1994). The postcolonial aura: Third world criticism in the age of global capitalism. *Critical Inquiry, 20*(2), 328–356.

Dyson, A. (1997). Writing superheroes. New York: Teachers College Press.

Fanon, F. (1963). *The wretched of the earth.* New York: Grove Press.

Fine, M. (1992). *Disruptive voices.* Ann Arbor: University of Michigan Press.

Fontana, A., & Frey, J. H. (1994). Interviewing: The art of science. In N. Denzin & Y. Lincoln (Eds.), *Handbook of qualitative research* (pp. 361–376). Thousand Oaks, CA: Sage.

Foucault, M. (1980). *Power/knowledge: Selected interviews and other writings 1972–1977.* New York: Pantheon.

Gitlin, A., Siegel, M., & Boru, K. (1989). The politics of method: From leftist ethnography to educative research. *Qualitative Studies in Education, 2,* 237–253.

Gordon, D. (Ed.). (1988). *Real and imagined women.* London: Routledge.

Hatch, J. A. (1995). Ethical conflicts in classroom research: Examples from a study of peer stigmatization in kindergarten. In J. A. Hatch (Ed.), *Qualitative research in early childhood settings* (pp. 213–223). Westport, CT: Praeger.

Hauser, M. (1995). Life history of a first grade teacher: A narrative of culturally sensitive practice. In J. A. Hatch (Ed.), *Qualitative research in early childhood settings* (pp. 63–78). Westport, CT: Praeger.

Jacoby, R. (1995, September/October). Marginal returns: The trouble with postcolonial theory. *Lingua Franca,* pp. 30–37.

Jipson, J., & Paley, N. (1997). *Daredevil research: Re-creating analytic practice.* New York: Peter Lang.

Johnson, R. (1997). The "no tough" policy. In J. Tobin (Ed.), *Making a place for pleasure in early childhood education* (pp. 101–118). New Haven: Yale University Press.

Kessen, W. (1979). The American child and other cultural inventions. *American Psychologist, 34*(10), 26–39.

Kumar, K. (1993). Study of childhood and family. In T. S. Saraswathi & B. Kaur (Eds.), *Human development and family studies in India* (pp. 67–76). New Delhi: Sage.

Lather, P. A. (1997). *Troubling the angels: Women living with HIV/AIDS.* Boulder, CO: Westview Press.

Misri, U. (1986). Child and childhood: A conceptual construction. In V. Das (Ed.), *The word and the world: Fantasy, symbol and record* (pp. 115–132). New Delhi: Sage.

Mongia, P. (1996). Introduction. In P. Mongia (Ed.), *Contemporary postcolonial theory: A reader* (pp. 1–19). London: Arnold.

Murphy, L. B. (1953). Roots of tolerance and tensions in Indian child development. In G. Murphy (Ed.), *In the minds of men* (pp. 46–58). New York:
Basic Books.

Olesen, V. (1994). Feminisms and models of qualitative research. In N. Denzin & Y. Lincoln (Eds.), *Handbook of qualitative research* (pp. 158–174).
Thousand Oaks, CA: Sage.

Reinharz, S. (1992). *Feminist methods in social research*. New York: Oxford
University Press.

Spivak, G. C. (1996). Poststructuralism, marginality, postcoloniality and value.
In P. Mongia (Ed.), *Contemporary postcolonial theory: A reader* (pp. 198–
223). London: Arnold.

Spradley, J. P. (1980). *Participant observation*. Fort Worth, TX: Harcourt Brace
Jovanovich.

Tobin, J., & Davidson, D. (1990). The ethics of polyvocal ethnography: Empowering vrs. textualizing children and teachers. *International Journal of
Qualitative Studies in Education, 3*, 271–284.

Trawick, M. (1990). *Notes on love in a Tamil family*. Berkeley: University of
California Press.

Walkerdine, V. (1984). Developmental psychology and the child-centered pedagogy: The insertion of Piaget into early childhood education. In J. Henriques, W. Holloway, C. Urwin, C. Venn, & V. Walkerdine (Eds.), *Changing the subject: Psychology, social regulation and subjectivity* (pp.
153–202). London: Methuen.

Walkerdine, V. (1997). *Daddy's girl*. Cambridge, MA: Harvard University
Press.

Wolf, M. (1992). *A thrice told tale: Feminism, postmodernism and ethnographic responsibility*. Stanford: Stanford University Press.

Woodhead, M. (1990). Psychology and the cultural construction of children's
needs. In A. James & A. Prout (Eds.), *Constructing and reconstructing
childhood* (pp. 60–78). New York: Falmer.

Identities and Possibilities

Gaile S. Cannella & Susan Grieshaber

RECONCEPTUALISTS AND postmodernist theories and/or perspectives avoid prescriptive information on classroom methodologies, guidelines for how to work with any particular group of people, or any type of "what works" or "effective practice" jargon that is so common in our educational discourse. Views of the world that challenge universal truths or grand narratives, make every attempt to avoid such "officialese" as well as the construction of alternative truth(s). For example, such terms as *effective practice*, while appearing objective and scientific, are charged with political, social, historical, contextual, and even gendered bias: What are the dominant cultural values of a context in which the term *effective* is considered important? Who decides what is meant by *effective*? Whose knowledge, skills, and beliefs are included? Whose strengths and abilities are excluded? Are particular ways of living in the world and learning privileged by the concept? Does the notion of *effective* create power for one group over another? Has the concept changed over time? Who is helped and who is hurt through the discourse and implementation of *effective practice*?

Educators and others who would challenge predetermined truths, including our rights as human beings to impose universalized truth(s) on others, must be steadfast in critiquing all discourses, including their own. For this reason, views of the world that are postmodern, reconceptualist, or have an affinity for the postmodern often are dismissed as providing no alternatives, as too theoretical or idealistic at best, and as nihilistic, dangerous, tearing everything apart, damaging, and even elitist at worst (to use modernist dualistic language). Reconceptualist views do not fit into modernist ways of approaching the world (e.g., discovering truth(s); thinking logically, linearly, and dichotomously; saving those pitiable "others" who are just not as intelligent, beautiful, or hardworking as the rest of society). We, however, believe that postmodernist, reconceptualist, challenge-to-truth orientations offer unlimited possibilities. As Richard Johnson proposed in Chapter 2, "This reconceptualist movement revels in the notion of possibility making."

The reluctance to impose truth on others and the openness to possibility have caused many reconceptualist researchers and scholars to be accused of ignoring the real world of teachers and children in classrooms. We and our colleagues are not disregarding teachers or the young people that they work with every day. We believe that giving some type of "postmodern model or methodology" would, however, be contrary to the very issues we raise. General possibilities that we see as directly applicable to classroom practice are similar to those raised by Rebecca Kantor and David Fernie in Chapter 2. These potential practices include: (1) recognition of the complexities and biases in society and that teachers cannot ignore the ways that societal power is exhibited in classrooms; (2) the use of genuine, equitable collaboration that includes children and their families in the creation of practices of education and care; and (3) actions taken based on collaboratively constructed values that are recognized as flexible and biased and are always examined for who is being heard, disqualified, helped, and hurt. These broad-based practices, in particular contexts, would lead to more specific actions. The authors in this book have provided many specific examples as beginning points for those who wish to take a critical postmodernist stance in their teaching, research, and service to/for young children.

RECONCEPTUALIZATION AND THE CLASSROOM

Directions for practice illustrated in this volume are multidimensional and include teachers, educational methods and content, as well as reconceptualization of dominant constructs in the field that traditionally have "informed" practice. Some possibilities involve teachers in rethinking who they are, how society has affected the way they feel about themselves and children, and the cultural context of the school. Teaching content and methods are addressed by introducing possibilities that can be used in classrooms, without requiring the teacher to reconceptualize everything in the room at once. Finally, long-term possibilities are presented for rethinking the major constructs that dominate education.

Teacher Identities

Teacher identities are explored from multiple vantage points (Chapters 3–5) in ways that expand understandings of the contexts and situations in which teachers find themselves as human beings. As one teacher said to me (Cannella), "Now that I examine the roles in my school, I understand that my discomfort wasn't my imperfection, but the atmosphere in which the principal was our father and we as teachers were to do as he said." Postmodernist examination of teaching reveals the modernist desires that emerge in teachers (especially women) to please everyone, save all the children, and learn exactly all the right actions and methods.

In Chapter 3 Sharon Ryan, Mindy Ochsner, and Celia Genishi address the limits placed on teacher identity when constructed within the boundaries of developmentally appropriate/inappropriate. They demonstrate how poststructuralism creates avenues for interpreting and problematizing identities within the political and historical context of education, from positions that reveal complexity and multiplicity.

Further, in contrasting the literatures on child advocacy and early childhood education, Sue Grieshaber in Chapter 4 illustrates the contradictions in identity that teachers face and that commonly are found also in societal messages to women in general. The advocate is to be critical, confrontational, and willing to negotiate arguments. The early childhood educator is to quietly care and nurture, to passively facilitate development. The possibilities for multiple and contradictory identities are obvious.

As Janice Kroeger demonstrates in Chapter 5, even a teacher who focuses on equity and social justice learned that the context of child/family/community survival in a particular situation required that she question her own notions of openness and justice. Even with her multiple lived experiences tied to gender (e.g., diversity, orientation, equity) and her dedication to social reconstructionism, she questioned herself as a teacher when faced with a contradiction—the conflict between Caleb's family and her perception of classroom transformational practice. The most historically, politically, and contextually astute teacher cannot entirely escape the remnants of societal gendering or modernist messages found throughout education and perpetuated in higher education (especially in teacher "training"). A "will to perfection" (determined by modernist society) as a teacher, and possibly as a woman, is strong.

Engagement with postmodernist and reconceptualist perspectives provides teachers with ways to understand themselves as socially, historically, and politically embedded. Rather than creating a will to perfection that can result only in feelings of inadequacy and failure, the complexities of identities and the ways that these identities are tied to society, power, and circumstance can be unveiled. Further, understanding ways that teaching can be contradictory, ambiguous, and highly influenced by the context in which teachers, children, and families are expected to survive, introduces identities that are temporally interrelated and dependent.

Postmodern attention to the historical, political, and societal grounding of individuals and groups can provide teachers with the freedom to resist the disciplinary and regulatory powers that limit them to one view of the "good teacher," the "professional worker," or the "perfect woman." We believe that all teacher educators, inservice teachers, and preservice teachers would benefit from learning about and respectfully considering postmodernist and reconceptualist positions as tied to their everyday lives.

Reconceptualized Content and Methods

Both educational content (knowledges) and methods of teaching are fertile areas for reconceptualization (as demonstrated in Chapters 6–8), especially as teachers begin to actually consider the everyday lived experiences of the younger people that they teach. Children are born into historical, political, social, and cultural contexts. Most live in a world with other human beings that are diverse and complex, and they do not escape or avoid these complexities just because they are young or are attending school. Teachers who recognize the complexities of children as human beings who are members of complicated, heterogeneous societies, can learn to see, talk to, and provide learning experiences that increase possibilities rather than limiting children to narrow discourses, control, and confined identities.

The introduction of multiple interpretations of child observation by Sheralyn Campbell and Kylie Smith (Chapter 6) is a very practical example of reconceptualizing methods and shifting identities. When a teacher no longer believes that she or he holds the truth about a child (the "truth" of developmental stage, characteristic, or progress), the teacher can be more open to possibilities. Rather than "seeing" the child as a bundle of developmental characteristics who will mature into an adult, the child can be seen as another human being who is too complex to understand or to label in any specific way (and, we would add, why would one person believe he or she has the human right to simplify others by assuming understanding anyway?). The child, as with any other person, can be seen as another human being with whom the teacher hopes to make connections. Further, recognizing that diverse philosophical views of life and societal experiences influence what is seen, a teacher can reverse the perspectives that dominate observation, creating new teaching tools. As examples, rather than making judgments about the developmental level of children, a teacher can use observation to (1) focus on his or her own teacher biases to determine whose knowledges, ideas, and life experiences are missing in the classroom; and (2) encourage children to explore multiple ways of seeing what happens in their interactions with each other.

Examples of knowledge that is part of the everyday lives of all young children are sexuality and popular culture, knowledge that can be unveiled and recognized as part of classroom culture and practice. As Rachel Theilheimer and Betsy Cahill illustrate in Chapter 7, messages concerning our expectations regarding sexuality for ourselves and others are found in the way we talk to children and make assumptions about their behavior. Heteronormative language and conclusions sanction only a narrow range of identities, disqualifying those who do not fit the norm, masking complex feelings, and even limiting those who fit the norm. Very minor changes in language can broaden the range of acceptances and possibilities. For example, even if a teacher is not yet fully comfortable with more open language, changing a statement like, "Boys who play with dolls won't be gay" to "Both boys and girls seem to really enjoy pretending with dolls," changes the message. Other examples of knowledge that can be greatly influenced by the assumptive messages in our language are gendering, privileging the "intellectual," and the discourse that gives power to reading over other skills.

Popular culture is an ever-changing knowledge base that is perhaps the most familiar for twenty-first-century children. The reactions of many of us to this popular culture has been either that it controls lives or that individuals can choose what is good or bad from the possibilities, as explained in the reaction to Barbie described by Patrick Hughes and Glenda Mac Naughton in Chapter 8. Further, many educators do everything possible to eliminate popular culture from the classroom. Reconceptualist and postmodernist perspectives do not delete knowledge, but recognize the complexity of roles and identities tied to that knowledge. Further, children are viewed as people who can analyze and critique the artifacts and products of their culture(s), who can explore with teachers the multiple motives, agendas, and possibilities found in a particular form of knowledge.

Identity Disruption

Challenging the existence of predetermined truth opens the door for the reconceptualization of constructs that dominate education, including early childhood education. In Chapters 9–11, the authors reveal issues regarding curriculum, ethnicity, and even the broad belief in research. Jenny Ritchie in Chapter 9 disrupts the individualistic identity of curriculum, proposing a more collectivist conceptualization. However, within the construct, she integrates content and methods that have emerged within the modernist institution, practices like role play and philosophical teaming, that are consistent with collectivism.

Just as Mäori perspectives would lead to a reconceptualization of curriculum purposes, content, and methods, there are no limits to the ways that curriculum may be (re)conceptualized. For example, as child development has been challenged as a knowledge base, one of the major questions from early childhood educators has been, "If not child development, what do we learn and teach about?" There are no limits to the possibilities as evidenced by the Latino community worker in San Antonio, Texas, who recently said, "Our grandmothers share all kinds of ideas, information, and experiences with us. We learn so much about our own culture." The curriculum theory scholars have already demonstrated to us that curriculum is autobiography; is gendered, racial, and religious texts; is certainly cultural; and can have no boundaries. We would be the first to recognize the political, power, and dominant-culture issues tied to curriculum (and that those issues must be strategically addressed). However, the reconceptualization of the purposes, content, and methods of curriculum is limited only by what we are willing to consider.

The disruption of ethnic identity, as illustrated by Susan Matoba Adler in Chapter 10, provides teachers with ways of approaching race, gender, ethnicity, and other dominant identity constructs from a historical, contextual perspective. Knowledge of the real-life experiences of others, both currently and historically, becomes a vehicle for openness to diverse identities, to shifting perspectives, and to the creation of possibilities.

The postcolonial challenge to research as a truth-oriented construct, introduced by Radhika Viruru and Gaile Cannella in Chapter

11, demonstrates that even our taken-for-granted, unquestioned ways of functioning (ways that some believe have been/are good for everyone) represent one view of the world and most likely privilege those who have the most power. For example, people of color, women, and minorities in various contexts have been labeled as deficient, lacking in skills, and irrational. Further, teachers who have connected as human beings with children have always challenged positivist testing and research as unrelated to the lives and abilities of the human beings that they know and respect. Research as a construct should be questioned, and, if used (perhaps because of political contexts or circumstance), at least reconceptualized to include multiple voices, flexibility, and a continued challenge to the imposition of research on others as truth.

Reconceptualist and postmodern perspectives would disrupt the identities of the field of education, as well as curriculum, research, methods, and people themselves. Within the context of disruption, possibilities are no longer confined. One such possibility is to reconceptualize the field of early childhood education to create a fluid, open field of childhood studies that includes developmental psychology but also invites and welcomes cultural studies, neocolonial studies, feminisms, and others, and that opens doors to legal, business, literature, and medical studies not only as playing significant roles in the lives of those who are younger, but as constructing views of those lives. A field of childhood studies without boundaries would challenge the separation of adult and child, but would also continue to foster the recognition that those who are younger have been oppressed and have not had power or been heard. As has so often been expressed about women's studies (Butler, 1990), those who are younger deserve political and linguistic visibility, legitimacy, and representation. The participants in the reconceptualized field could engage in all forms of critical, political activism. Most important, a reconceptualized field could focus on collaboration with those who are younger, their families, and their communities, learning how to connect as human beings without predetermined psychological or gendered expectations. Reconceptualizing of the field as postmodernist childhood studies is just one possibility. We would challenge the reader to generate many others.

SHIFTED IDENTITIES

Even if teachers do not reject modernism, renounce DAP, expand views of younger human beings, or reconceptualize classroom practices, we suggest that a thorough and fair consideration of reconceptualist, postmodernist perspectives can expand a person's thoughts and feelings about society, about his or her own life, and about the lives of others. Consideration of even one of the following can open the door to the reconstruction of identities and multiple possibilities:

- Truth as inequitable imposition on others
- Societal issues of race, gender, economics, and power as always present, even in classrooms
- Challenges to the taken for granted
- Multiple ways of living and being in the world
- Life as a struggle (not read as a negative) with other beings
- Collaboration that constructs values, but engages in continual critique

Finally, we ask the modernist question, "How do reconceptualist, postmodernist discourses and actions result in positive change for children, their families, and/or their teachers?" We respond by calling attention to the complexity that is our lives and the diversity that constitutes our identities. We cannot ultimately know whether our beliefs, ideas, and practices have a positive impact. Massive actions like the construction of Head Start literally may have "saved" some individuals, yet may have perpetuated deficit perspectives in ways that have permanently damaged others. Postmodernist feminism may be taught for years to inservice teachers and appear to have no effect on the classroom, yet an individual in one of those classrooms may use the conversations 5 years later to support her actions in leaving an abusive husband. We cannot predict outcomes or even determine their possibilities. We can only work together to continually act on our values, while at the same time placing those values under perpetual critique.

Reconceptualist, postmodernist views of the world are not prescriptive, do not claim to be determinism. For early childhood education, the perspectives can be and are tied to diversity, flexibility, and critique—to the construction of shifting and reinvented identities that are willing to turn their own worlds upside down to reinvent and increase possibilities with/for those who are younger. We do not engage in a battle for the "right" way to conceptualize understanding. We want to engage in a lifelong struggle to unveil unthought-of possibilities for all of us.

REFERENCE

Butler, J. (1990). *Gender trouble: Feminism and the subversion of identity.* London: Routledge.

About the Editors and Contributors

Susan Grieshaber is a Principal Researcher at the Centre for Applied Studies in Early Childhood and a Senior Lecturer in the School of Early Childhood, Queensland University of Technology, Brisbane, Australia. She has wide experience as an early childhood teacher in urban and rural communities and has worked with children and families from a diversity of contexts, including Aboriginal children, children from non-English-speaking families, children with disabilities, and children and families from all socioeconomic backgrounds. Dr. Grieshaber's research interests include early childhood curriculum, families, and gender. She also has written about policy in early childhood education.

Gaile S. Cannella is an Associate Professor in the Department of Educational Psychology at Texas A&M University. She is a former early childhood and elementary teacher who received a master's degree from Tennessee Technological University and a doctoral degree from the University of Georgia. Dr. Cannella has served on the faculties of Louisiana State University, the University of Northern Iowa, and St. John's University in New York. She is the author of *Deconstructing Early Childhood Education: Social Justice and Revolution* and currently is co-editing (with Joe Kincheloe) the book *Kidworld: Childhood Studies, Global Perspectives, and Education* and co-authoring (with Radhika Viruru) *Childhood and (Post)Colonization: Power, Education, and Contemporary Practice.* Her interests are the construction of a broad-based field of "childhood studies" that includes critical advocacy, poststructural and feminist perspectives, and recognition of political, historical, cultural, and linguistic contexts. Dr. Cannella has also worked (with Rafael Lara-Alecio) in the Texas A&M University BIL/ESL Childhood Studies Grants Program, which focuses on engaging teachers from a variety of backgrounds and life circumstances in child/family/community advocacy regarding linguistic/cultural diversity and educational support.

Susan Matoba Adler is an Assistant Professor of Early Childhood Education in the Department of Curriculum and Instruction, University of Illinois at Urbana–Champaign. She received her Ph.D. from the University of Wisconsin–Madison in 1995, and her book, titled *Mothering Ethnicity and Education: The Transformation of Japanese American Culture*, was released in 1998. Previously, she was a member of the faculty at the University of Michigan–Ann Arbor and Flint, teaching early childhood education courses at the graduate and undergraduate levels. Her research focuses on the racial and ethnic identity development of Asian American children and home–school relations with Asian American families.

Betsy Cahill is an Associate Professor and Coordinator of Early Childhood Teacher Education at New Mexico State University. Prior to receiving her Ph.D. from Kent State University, she was a teacher of young children for 14 years. Her primary research interest is the intersection of gender and sexual identity development in children, with a particular focus on heteronormative expectations. Rachel Theilheimer and Betsy have collaborated on numerous articles and book chapters on the subject.

Sheralyn Campbell is a Ph.D. student and Lecturer at the University of Melbourne, Department of Learning and Educational Development. She has worked in a range of early childhood services within the Australian context and been involved in training early childhood teacher education students. She is currently a member of an action research team working at the University of Melbourne, Swanston Street Children's Centre. Her research interests are materialized in questions about how early childhood theory and practice can be reconceptualized in ways that improve how social justice and equity operate for staff, students, families, and children in child-care services.

David E. Fernie is Professor of Early Childhood Education in the College of Education at Ohio State University. He obtained his B.A. (cum laude) from Harvard College and his Ed.D. from the University of Massachusetts at Amherst. His interests include the multiple meanings of children's play, children's understanding and uses of media/technology, and the ethnographic study of early educational settings and processes. He is the former Chair of the Early Education and Child Development Special Interest Group of AERA and is Co-Principal Investigator of the Region Vb Head Start Qnet, a training and technical assistance organization serving Head Start grantees in Indiana, Illinois, and Ohio.

Celia Genishi is Professor of Education in the Department of Curriculum and Teaching at Teachers College, Columbia University. She is a former secondary Spanish and preschool teacher and now teaches courses related to early childhood education and qualitative research methods. She completed her doctoral work at the University of California, Berkeley (Ph.D., 1976) and was on the faculties at the University of Texas at Austin and Ohio State University. She is co-author (with Anne Haas Dyson) of *Language Assessment in the Early Years,* editor of *Ways of Assessing Children and Curriculum,* and co-editor (with Anne Haas Dyson) of *The Need for Story: Cultural Diversity in Classroom and Community.* She is the recipient of a Distinguished Scholar Award (1996) from the American Educational Research Association and an Advocate for Justice Award from the American Association of Colleges for Teacher Education (1998). Her research interests include collaborative research with teachers on alternative assessments, childhood bilingualism, and classroom discourse.

J. Amos Hatch is Professor of Inclusive Early Childhood Education at the University of Tennessee. He has worked in early childhood education for almost 30 years and holds degrees from the University of Utah, University of North Florida, and University of Florida. Dr. Hatch has published numerous articles and chapters in areas of concern to early childhood professionals. He also has served as editor of *Qualitative Studies in Education* and of two books related to qualitative research in early childhood settings. He currently is working with colleagues in Australia on a study of early childhood teachers' work and completing a qualitative research methods book to be published in 2001.

Patrick Hughes is a Lecturer in Communications at Deakin University, Australia. Previously, he taught media and cultural studies at London University and the Open University in the UK; he has acted as a communications consultant to public and private organizations in both Australia and the UK. He has a B. Tech (Honors) degree from Brunel University and a Ph.D. from London University. His major research interest is the industrialization and commodification of communication and culture, with particular focus on professional communication and the representation and marketing of science. His work has been published as books and articles in Australia, the UK, and the United States, and is included in *Media International Australia Incorporating Culture and Policy* and *The Politics of Early Childhood Education* (edited by Lourdes Diaz Soto). Together, he and Glenda Mac Naughton have published *Communication in Early Childhood Services: A Practical Guide.*

Janice A. Jipson is Professor of Education at National Louis University. She received her doctorate in curriculum and instruction from the University of Wisconsin. She is co-editor (with Joe Kincheloe) of the academic book series Rethinking Childhood for Peter Lang Publishing. Her own recent books include *Resistance and Representation: Rethinking Childhood* (with Richard Johnson), *Questions of You and the Struggle of Collaborative Life* (with Nicholas Paley), *Intersections: Feminisms/Early Childhoods* (with Mary Hauser), *Daredevil Research: Re-Creating Analytic Practice* (with Nicholas Paley), and *Repositioning Feminism and Education: Perspectives on Educating for Social Change* (with Petra Munro).

Richard Johnson, a former preschool teacher, received his Ed.D. from George Peabody College, Vanderbilt University, specializing in early childhood education. After working for several years at the University of Houston, he is now a Professor in the Department of Teacher Education and Curriculum Studies, University of Hawai'i at Manoa. His most recent research focuses on the implications of risk in early education, specifically "no touch" policies on the care of young children, a book appearing as *Hands Off! The Disappearance of Touch in the Care of Children.* Further, his co-edited book *Resistance and Representation: Rethinking Early Childhood* was just released.

Rebecca Kantor is Professor of Early Childhood Education in the College of Education at Ohio State University. Prior to holding a faculty position in the College of Education, she was on the faculty in the College of Human Ecology at OSU where she also served as Director of the A. Sophie Rogers Lab School for 14 years. She obtained her B.A. from the University of Rochester and her M.Ed. in early childhood education and Ed.D. in language and cognition from Boston University. Her research interests revolve around social processes in early childhood settings, including language, literacy, and children's friendships and peer cultures. She is Co-Principal Investigator of the Region Vb Head Start Qnet, a training and technical assistance organization serving Head Start grantees in Indiana, Illinois, and Ohio.

Janice Kroeger is presently a doctoral candidate in curriculum and instruction at the University of Wisconsin–Madison. Her past experiences include advocacy/care/education of young children within lab school and compensatory programs. Her current research interests stem from theorizing about inclusive understandings of diversity and identity in the early childhood classroom. She is interested in processes of cultural change for social and educational equity, the bidirectional processes of relationships between families and schools, and qualitative methodologies. Her doctoral dissertation examines the experiences of families and educators in the early primary grades within home and school relationships.

Glenda Mac Naughton gained her doctorate from Deakin University and has worked in the early childhood field for nearly 28 years. She is currently an Associate Professor in the Faculty of Education at the University of Melbourne. Her years in early childhood have included work as a practitioner, a manager, and a senior policy advisor to government in the UK and Australia. She currently is involved in a major review of early childhood curriculum in Tasmania and in facilitating a critical teaching project for the Department of Education in South Australia. Dr. Mac Naughton has a passionate interest in social justice and equity issues in early childhood and has published widely on these issues nationally and internationally. Her two most recently published books are being used throughout Australia and deal with approaches to teaching in early childhood and communication in early childhood services.

Mindy Ochsner earned her Ed.D. at Teachers College, Columbia University, in New York City. As an Assistant Professor, she teaches undergraduate and graduate early childhood courses at Rhode Island College. Her research interests include exploring gender from feminist poststructuralist perspectives. Presently, she is the principal investigator of a collaborative research project made possible in part by the Spencer Foundation and the Rhode Island College Faculty Research Fund entitled "Locating, Sustaining, and Disrupting Gender Discourses: A Feminist Poststructuralist Study of Gender in Three Kindergarten Classrooms."

Jenny Ritchie is a Senior Lecturer in the Early Childhood Studies Department at the University of Waikato, Hamilton, Aotearoa/New Zealand. She has been involved in early childhood care and education since the late 1970s as a child-care worker, kindergarten teacher, Playcentre parent, and *Kōhanga Reo whānau* member. She and her partner are raising six children who are bilingual in English and Māori. Her qualifications were obtained from Hamilton Teachers College and the University of Waikato. Her current research involves developing understandings of the ways in which a mainstream New

Zealand teacher education program prepares teachers to deliver a bi-cultural early childhood curriculum.

Sharon Ryan is an Assistant Professor of Early Childhood Education in the Graduate School of Education at Rutgers University. Before moving to the United States to undertake graduate studies at Teachers College, Columbia University, Dr. Ryan was a preschool teacher, special education adviser, early childhood consultant, and lecturer in South Australia. Her main research interests include investigating the theories of classroom teachers, equitable approaches to educating young students, and the potential of alternative theories for reconceptualizing early childhood education in theory, research, and practice. As part of this work, she recently has begun work on a qualitative study of how a group of teachers and their students enact and experience a statewide preschool policy. Some of her publications include "Traditional Practices, New Possibilities: Transforming Dominant Images of Early Childhood Teachers," co-authored with Mindy Ochsner, and "Does Theory Lead Practice? Teachers' Constructs About Teaching: Top-Down Perspectives," co-authored with Fran Schoonmaker.

Kylie Smith is currently Director of the Swanston Street Children's Centre at the University of Melbourne and has experience in a variety of Australian early childhood services. She is also a Ph.D. student at the University of Melbourne, Department of Learning and Educational Development. Her research interests include how theory and practice can challenge and change how equity operates in the early childhood classroom.

Rachel Theilheimer is an Associate Professor of Early Childhood Education at the Borough of Manhattan Community College, City University of New York. She received a master's degree from Bank Street College of Education and an Ed.D. from Teachers College, Columbia University. She has worked as a teacher and director with children ranging in age from 6 months to 9 years. Her research interests focus on early childhood teacher education, with specific interest in issues related to social justice. She has written several articles and book chapters with Betsy Cahill on the relationship between children's eventually emerging sexual identities, early childhood curriculum, and teacher education.

Radhika Viruru received her Ph.D. in education from Texas A&M University where she is a Lecturer in Early Childhood Education. Her book *Decolonizing Early Childhood Education: An Indian Perspective* is currently in press. Additionally, Dr. Viruru is co-editor (with Gaile

Cannella) of the section "Childhood and Cultural Studies," published in the *Journal of Curriculum Theorizing*. Her research interests and publications address issues of postcolonial theory and its relationship to early childhood education. She is currently writing *Childhood and (Post) Colonization: Power, Education, and Contemporary Practice* with Gaile Cannella.

Index

"Historical child". *See* Caleb
Holloway, W., 95
Homophobia, 18, 104, 105, 106, 107
Homosexuality, 103–11. *See also* Lesbians
Horvatt, M., 75
Howes, C., 49–50
Hughes, Patrick, 18, 114–30, 177–78
Hulsebosch, P., 75
Humanism, 65, 66, 118

Identity
  and constructions that limit education,
    15–17
  desire in creation of, 123
  disruption, 178–79
  of field of early childhood education,
    13
  individual, 8–9
  as multiple, contradictory, and dynamic, 122–24
  and new models of identity formation,
    127–28
  as political issue, 121, 122, 127, 128
  and possibilities, 173–80
  and shifted identities, 179–80
  See also specific topic
India, colonialism/postcolonialism in, 13,
    18, 19, 158, 159, 162–63, 164, 167
Individual identities, 8–9
Individualism
  and collectivism, 142
  and modernism, 6, 7
  New Right, 18–19, 133–35, 138, 140,
    144–45
  and race/ethnicity, 151–52
Instrumentalism, 151
Intelligences, inter– and intra–personal,
    137–38
Irwin, D. M., 91
Italy, teacher training in, 38–39

Jacoby, R., 158
James, A., 3, 89
Japanese Americans, identity and voice
  of, 18, 19, 148–57
Jarvis, B., 41
Jenks, C., 3, 89
Jipson, Janice A., 28–35, 41, 42, 169

Joan (lesbian parent), 74, 75–80, 81, 82,
  83–84
Johnson, R., 29, 39–41, 42, 168, 174
Jonathan (child of lesbian parents), 76–
  77, 78, 79, 80, 81, 82
Jones, E., 136
Jones, M., 115

Kantor, Rebecca, 35–39, 41, 42, 174
Katz, L., 90, 142–43, 144
Kellner, D., 4, 8, 9, 10, 13, 65
Kessen, W., 161
Kessler, Shirley, 3, 28–29
Kilpatrick, William, 30
King, J. R., 109, 110
Kingsolver, Barbara, 133
Kitano, H. L., 152
Knowledge, 6–9, 10, 11, 47, 52, 63, 158,
  167, 176–78
Koerner, M., 75
Köhanga Reo movement, 134, 139, 140,
  142
Kroeger, Janice, 16–17, 73–86, 175–76
Kuhn, T. S., 3
Kumar, K., 163

Ladson-Billings, G., 152, 155–56
Lam, Lamson (graduate student), 153,
  154
Lambert, B., 90, 91
Language, 6, 17, 66–67, 177
Lareau, A., 75
Lather, Patti, 10, 52, 166
Learning, 7, 117, 118, 167
Leavitt, Robin, 3–4, 11–12, 136
Lee, Stacey, 151, 155
Leonardo, Zeuss, 134–35
Lesbians
  ignorances, silences, and assumptions
    about, 103–9, 110–11
  and lesbian family in classroom, 73–
    86, 175–76
  and postmodern shifting identities,
    16–17
Levin, N., 116
Lewis, M., 108
Lindamood, J. B., 61
Lindauer, S., 141
Liu, K., 138, 143, 144
Lively, E., 108